The Ring

Written By:

Romaro A. Green & Clarissa L. Green

Published by Unbreakable Book Publishing Clarissa Green, Editor-in-Chief

Copyright © 2018 Romaro A. Green. Clarissa L. Green.

All rights reserved. No part of this publication may be reproduced, distributed, or transmitted in any form or by any means, including photocopying, recoding, or other electronic or mechanical methods without written permission from the authors except in the case of brief quotations embodied in critical reviews and certain noncommercial uses permitted by copyright law.

Disclaimer: This book is not an evidence-based approach to marriage counseling and has not been approved or certified by any federal, state or local agencies or facility programs. Neither author is certified nor licensed in family or marriage counseling. All commentaries in this book are based on personal experiences and theories.

First printing February 2018.
Written by Romaro A. Green, Clarissa L. Green

Edited by Clarissa L. Green
Cover Photo Designed by Clarissa L. Green, Created by David Edwards Jr.

Published by Unbreakable Publishing Company, LLC
Milwaukee, WI
Sole Proprietress Clarissa L. Green

Copyright © 2018 Romaro Green, Clarissa Green
All rights reserved.

ISBN-10: 0692061029
ISBN-13: 978-0692061022

The Ring

By: Romaro & Clarissa Green

FOREWORD

By Dr. Dwayne McAlister SR;
Doctorate in Divinity,
Master in Christian Counseling,
Bachelor's in theology

The wedding ring is a significant part of a marriage ceremony. Marriage is honorable. The analogue of the ring shows how our father God intended a union to be.

First of all, the ring is circle which indicates neither a beginning nor an end. Marriage is continuous work, play and love. Secondly, the gold or silver has been tried in the fire. The fire is a purifier and it hardens it. Sometimes marriage goes through a purification process to make you strong for one another. Lastly, the diamonds in the ring. The diamonds are cut and set by a gemologist. It takes a trained eye to set diamonds. The cutting and setting of the diamonds are designed so it glistens no matter how you view it.

So, it is with marriage, times it may have to be cut and set so that all may see the beauty and glistening of marriage. Let God work in your marriage continuously. Allow Him to try your marriage with fire. Remember that the cut and set in your marriage serves a testimony to others.

"Love is a ~~beautiful~~ thing."

-Clarissa

Thing

[THiNG] 🔊

noun

An object that one need not, cannot, or does not wish to give a specific name or label to

CONTENTS

	Acknowledgments	Pg. viii
1	Intro: The Ring	Pg. 11
2	History: Green's Dark Secrets	Pg. 15
3	Communication	Pg. 23
4	Dirty Debate	Pg. 29
5	Prioritizing	Pg. 35
6	Step Parenting	Pg. 43
7	Love	Pg. 49
8	Lovemaking	Pg. 55
9	Home Improvement	Pg. 63
10	Social Media	Pg. 93
11	"I Do!" or... "Do I?"	Pg. 99
12	Wedding Vows	Pg. 101

ACKNOWLEDGMENTS

First and foremost, we would like to thank God for being the ruler of our lives, the head of our household and the chief of our marriage. God has played a major role in our desire to publish such intimate information. He gets all the glory for the messages brought forth throughout this book.

Next, we would like to express the unconditional love to all the children that we share from previous relationships and together: Kala, Boo, Man-Man, RJ, Cashae, Shala, Vonte, Mello & Essence. You all are loved deeply!

To our parents: Mae & Dennis, Missy & Silk, Wayne, and Zina: Thank you all for allowing such a union to come into fruition! Without your guidance, consent & blessings, we would not be where we are today.

Sincerest thanks to all our family and friends that support the various ministries we operate in and for the encouraging, inspiring words given whether it be colleagues, social media friends, acquaintances, etc. We appreciate the accolades and generosity you've all shown throughout the years.

From the KING Romaro: Every man must find the right woman and the woman that a man chooses will either catapult him into his destiny or tie him down to complacency. I thank God for not only blessing me with my Queen, but a God sent vessel to push me to do His mighty works here on earth to fulfill my destiny.

From the QUEEN Clarissa: Wow! I never imagined my life would be where it is and the direction it's headed. God was good to me when he sent me my mighty man of God! Nobody told me it would be easy, yet I'm a believer that I can do all things through Christ which strengthens me! And we'll stand firmly on the word of God til' eternity.

Special thanks to the supporters of Unbreakable Publishing! You all are amazing!!!

INTRO: THE RING

What's the first thing that comes to mind when you hear the word *"marriage"*? I'm sure most of you thought about the wedding. What factor, after the wedding, indicates that someone is married? You guessed it right again, the *ring*!

As depicted in the Foreword of this book, the ring is symbolic for an everlasting union. Let's be honest, a ring doesn't constitute a marriage, a commitment does.

We find ourselves not wearing our wedding ring more than we find ourselves with them on. The title of this book was inspired by that because for us, it's not about a tangible item, *"The Ring"*.

Let me introduce myself. I'm Clarissa Green, author of the book "Love Stings", sole proprietress of Unbreakable Publishing Company and the daughter of Dr. Dwayne McAlister Sr.
In this book, my husband Minister Romaro A. Green and I will share our opinions, philosophies and approach on the good, the bad and the indifferent associated with *"The Ring"*.

I can recall about nine years ago someone said, "Dang, he's old enough to be her daddy!" Someone said, "She's not even his main chick!" They called our relationship, "Just a fling." Now it's seven years later with a ring!

Seven is the biblical number of completion. God also communicates the number seven as perfection and wholeness.

For our seventh year anniversary, February 2018, we decided to renew our wedding vows. In doing so, we also selected such an occasion to launch this book, *"The Ring."*

Many who know us, been around us or have witnessed us interact on social media sites can attest that from the outside, we have a prosperous, humor-filled marriage. We support one another, uplift one another and often express our love for one another publicly.

In a sense you can say our marriage is like an open book. As Christians, we realize that any and every part of our story (or testimony), could be beneficial to someone else. It's been said many times that our connection is an inspiration to other couples.

I once read a quote that said something to the effect of, "All relationships go through hell; the real ones make it through it." Just like any good thing in life, there will be bad days, obstacles, trials and tribulations.

When these adversities ascend in a marriage, how do you face them together? What about when the adversities are against one another and things appear to be falling apart? How do you make it through? How can you defeat quandaries against your spouse or significant other without separating or getting that undesirable D-word also known as divorce?

I know, lots and lots of questions. Unfortunately, marriage didn't come with a participant guide or step by step instructions. It's not a black and white ordeal, it has many gray areas.

Not every couple has the combined skills to resolve issues and sort through the gray areas when needed. The goal of this book is to aid couples into conversations to recognize and resolve conflicts to improve their relationship and/or marriage.

We prayed for guidance as we wrote this book. Our prayer is that this book helps repair broken marriages, solidify the weak ones and impart eternity to the strong ones!

Many have that goal to be the perfect wife or the perfect husband with a happily everlasting marriage. Haha, everlasting not ever after, this isn't a fairy tale, it's real life!

But the focus should be on *how* to be a great wife and *how* to be a great husband versus actually being one. Perfection is flawless and in marriage, that's impractical.

> *"Too often we focus on who we want to be & where we want to be and lose sight on how to get there."*
> *– Clarissa*

It's safe to say that we must put more work in being the person we're aiming to be. That includes making sacrifices, adjustments, and exceptions. These things are not always easy to do.

Moving along, he say - she say has been famously known as gossip or hearing things from different sources without any reputable truths behind what's being heard. Well, we've decided to spread some he say - she say to our readers but in a different sense.

He say, is the opinions/theories of Romaro throughout this book. She say, is the opinions/theories of Clarissa. Not all topics are agreed upon, yet some views may be similar.

When preaching, Minister Romaro always advises to "pull out a no. 2 pencil and a highlighter", for listeners to take notes. Reason being, we only retain about 10% of what we read and 20% of what we hear.

Don't just read this book for entertainment or to support us on our new project but allow yourself and your spouse to grow from it. If you're not married yet, use it as a pre-martial tool.

Highlight great ideas, facts or concepts, discuss them with your significant other and effectively apply them to your relationship. Some things of course may be revised to fit your personal preference and that's perfectly fine by us.

HISTORY: THE GREEN'S DARK SECRETS

To know us, is to love us, to be one of our social media comrades, is to adore us! The cute, adorable moments haven't always been present. Just like all couples, we have disagreements and arguments.

In the past, others have gotten a thrill at our heated arguments or disagreements. At times, without filter, we'd exchange mean, greasy words to one another and people would just laugh. Not to make a mockery of us, but because an argument between the two of us can be quite enjoyable.

Without degrading one another, we'd make snide remarks back and forth. With our bubbly, comical personalities, it'd be naturally humorous and we'd both just laugh it off for the most part.

Via social media, we share plentiful events, occasions, and moments in our lives. We also publicly show gratitude towards one another sharing an array of occurrences and routine gestures which appear to be admirable to the average "Jill and Joe" or "Keisha and Kevin"; whichever way you deem fit.

One thing that the physical eye can attest to is our age gap. Later in this book, we just might reveal the exact number of years between us, for those that are dying to know.

Some may reckon that some of the details of our dark secrets we're "exposing" as TMI or too much information. However, we view them as being transparent. How can we expect others to learn from us without revealing our shortcomings? We prayed on these things and concluded that only God can pass judgment.

Rome and I met in June 2008 as co-workers. His generous gestures of allowing me to carpool to and from work with him, buying me lunch and conversing with me on a regular instantly became observant of the kind of man he was.

His conversations were always selfless. He showed lots of interest in me, my life, and my goals. We eventually started seeing one another outside of work and began casually dating.

An incident occurred with me on a night out on the town which led to me being treated at the emergency room. I called into work the next day and informed the manager that I'd be taking the day off.

When Rome arrived to work and learned of the news, he came to my sister's house to make sure I was okay. He didn't call or text, he showed up right on the doorstep and expressed great empathy of what had happened to me.

To be completely honest, I received an unpleasant shiner because of the incident. What did this gentleman Rome do? He supplied me with a pair of cheetah print, Rocawear sunglasses to conceal my injury.

From those moments, I knew there was something special about this man. He began to spoil me with compassion and money. Within five months, we took a big step, not knowing what was to come, and moved into an apartment together. Let me not fail to mention that I had been homeless, sleeping on my sister's couch and was seven months pregnant with my first child.

Now, for those of you that did the math, you read it correctly and your assumption is also correct. Yes, I was expecting when we met. And sadly, I was pregnant at the time I received that big black eye.

It was something he knew all along and accepted it. It's kind of, sort of uncommon for a pregnant gal to date another guy and even more uncommon for a guy to date a pregnant gal. But for us, there were no issues.

In all honesty, it was amazing! He'd accompany me to my routine doctor appointments, listen to me complain about the undesirable changes of my body due to pregnancy and do everything in his ability to make sure I stayed comfortable.

From purchasing an expensive heated massage pillow for work, to satisfying my daily food cravings, rubbing my aching feet and to top it off, he even attended Lamaze classes with me to prepare for childbirth. It's safe to say, he didn't miss a beat!

One month after moving in together, December 23rd, 2008, I gave birth to a healthy baby boy, Davonte Jr. Even though I was in this new relationship, I still named my son after his biological father. He was cordially accepting at the fact that I moved on quickly and that his first-born child would be residing in the household with another man.

At the hospital, we encountered some awkward moments. While my son's father was in the delivery room with me, Rome came to visit. The nurse knew that I was already accompanied by my son's father and anxiously alerted me that another guy claiming to be my significant other was in the waiting room, asking to enter.

Rome knew why the nurse was alarmed and hesitant about allowing him to visit. After I gave her the okay for him to come in, she escorted him to the room. She came to me, in front of both Rome and my son's father, and expressed why she didn't want to allow him to come in and apologized. The three of us all ensured her that it was completely understandable. We all got a good laughed at the situation.

Of course, many may have had opinions, whether they verbally expressed it directly to either of us, about us dating coming directly from other relationships. Sit tight; I'll introduce you to his other relationship prior to us in just a moment.

Nonetheless, we never cared what others thought or had to say, we were happy and in due time, everyone would attest to it.

On March 23, 2010, I gave birth to our first child in common, RoMello. Another wow moment, we didn't waste much time having a child together. If you're like me and mentally create a timeline to understand and analyze the chain of events, I'll help you out.

Rome and I met June 2008 while I was with child, moved in together November 2008, I had a child that is not biologically his December 2008 and we had a child together March 2010. My children were exactly fifteen months apart.

There you have it, you're welcome.

Going back, prior to the conception of our son RoMello, we endured some of the toughest times since the beginning of our relationship, up until the present time.

About a month after living together, I learned that Rome ended a longtime relationship the moment we moved in. In other words, he moved out from with her the same day we moved in together.

As we continued to cohabitate, many secrets surfaced showing that he was still involved with this other woman in which he had three children with.

We began to clash daily due to his unfaithfulness. It was some of the worst days of my life! Here I am, a new mother with my first home and my first relationship as an adult, and I was being lied to, cheated on and my heart was being crushed like never before.

The Ring

We'd get into arguments over his infidelities and he'd leave and go back to her. Meanwhile, I kept my doors open for him to come and go as he pleased. When he'd get into arguments with her due to continuing to deal with me, he'd leave her and come back to me. This common cycle in a broken home continued for months.

As bad as I needed to leave this toxic situation alone, I continued to accept it. At this time, I had no ties to him. I hadn't even known him a year, but my heart was in it deep.

Why aid me from homelessness, to put me in a position where you privately steal my peace, my joy and my sanity? He came in my life at one of my lowest points, took me to a peak of happiness, just to tear it all back down. I was better off when had nothing!

On one occasion, his kid's mother and I had an altercation which landed me in jail. I was devastated! I spent a week away from my son who was only six months old. I cried the entire time away. During those long six days, I broke down and told myself that I not only deserved better, but I'd be doing better once I was released.

When I got out of jail, Rome sat me down and expressed great empathy for what had happened. He took full responsibility for the consequences I had to suffer due to his lies and unfaithfulness. He ensured me, like many times before, that he would be loyal and stop going back and forth between the two of us.

Pleading for me to believe that he would no longer cheat was repetitive and a promise he had broken many times before. It went in one ear and out the other.

There was one thing that he said during this conversation that I hadn't heard before. It stood out and sent chills up my body and I took heed to it and never looked back.

Before I get into details, let me tell you all, my father is a

Pastor. So yeah, that makes me a "PK" or a preacher's kid. The dual-life stereotype that a preacher's daughter was religious but also lived a wild life, outside of the morals of religion was in fact, my truth. While all the turmoil was going on as I shacked up, I was still attending church regularly.

During these dark moments of secrecy, I prayed like never before. I prayed daily for God to give me the strength to walk away from the relationship that meant me no good. I knew that God wouldn't answer my prayers because I was putting him second to this man that was slowing shredding my heart into pieces.

During our conversation, Rome told me that while I was in jail, God spoke to him and he was ready to give his life to God. What stood out the most on this matter is the fact that I never forced religion on him. He was almost a middle-aged man, spent most of his life in the world doing worldly things.

At times he'd complain about me being committed to church and not wanting to miss service. He'd pout and get upset which would cause me to make the "sacrifice" not to attend. I didn't even bother ever asking him to go with me because it just wasn't his "MO".

But now, after all these years living for the world, he was ready to live for God! After the drama he and I had been through, this was the only thing that kept me from leaving him at this point. I knew that if we could both get on the same page spiritually, God would for sure oversee our relationship and things were bound to get better.

He began going to church with me instantaneously and eventually got saved, joined the church and became a minister. Since that conversation, July 2009, we've never crossed that dark path again. The road hasn't been easy but there has only been bumps in the roads and not road blocks.

If you've ever had a low moment in a relationship, you can truly value the high moments! There is no guarantee the contents of this book will assist anyone yet providing factual information and details of the many things we've overcome can definitely provide hope for those in similar situations.

"WE FOUGHT...

WE CRIED...

&

WE CONQUERED!

It was during one of our darkest moments when we encountered GROWTH."

-Mr. & Mrs. Green

COMMUNICATION

Prior to writing this book, we acknowledged the fact our communication could be a lot better when it came down to resolving issues whether big or small.

If there was something he had said or done that bothered me, it would be difficult to bring the issue up to discuss without it turning into an argument.

It wasn't often, however if I brought it up when we were at peace, he'd say I was ruining the mood. But when I brought it up when I was upset about a separate situation, it would add fuel to the fire and still wouldn't get extinguished.

When I brought this to his attention, he agreed that there had to be a better way to bring up any conflicts. He embraced the fact that I felt that I could never successfully get anything resolved with him.

We decided to schedule a time to resolve conflict and talk out any differences we had. About a year prior to this book coming out, God gave the concept to us. We began to utilize Thursdays at 6pm as a time to resolve any conflict that may be bothering us.

We agreed to listen to one another more and lay our guard down to avoid being defensive. We created rules to prevent the discussion from escalating to an argument. There could be no profanity due to the type of tone that may come across. Only one person could speak at a time. The other had to wait until the other person was done and verbalized that they were done.

There wasn't a time where we ended the discussion upset. We'd make sure to have a clear understanding of what needed to be done to satisfy each other's oppositions, if anything.

So often he'd say I'm against him when I expressed my opinions about a situation. This technique was different. During these arranged conversations, we concluded that just because we don't agree, doesn't mean that we're against one another.

It felt amazing to have an agreement as such! It was vital to communicating. It alleviated drama and misunderstandings.

If we can agree on anything in our marriage or in this book, we would say that communication is crucial to a successful marriage. Communication preserves the foundation, sets the tone and serves as the power source in a marriage.

One day, I created a post on a social media page for married couples. I simply asked what the most common obstacle that marriages face today. The top answer was simply, lack of communication.

Our marriage stands on honesty, trust and loyalty. We make it clear that we can verbally talk to one another at any given time, about any given subject.

The *master* key to communication in a marriage, surprisingly, is the listening segment. It has been said for decades that too often, we do not listen with the intent to understand but we listen with the intent to reply.

We felt that we both upheld that concept when communicating with one another. We had our own theory of how each other communicate and it wasn't pretty. He created acronyms from his perspective and I created one from mines.

He Say

Obliviously, you're not as smart as you think you are E=mc2 Einstein!
Nothing seems to penetrate through that big a** head of yours.
Everything does not have to go your way!

Sometimes you should consider taking your own advice.
Instigating conflict should not be at the top of your to-do list.
Don't start something you can't finish. It's my time to talk now!
Even though you are the loudest, it does not make your point correct.
Do you really think you're right about EVERYTHING?

Now fellas, I'm sure I'm not the only one with a one-sided, argumentative woman! They always think they know everything, they're quick to instigate an argument and truly believe that what they have to say in a conversation is right and we're wrong.

Or maybe, just maybe, it's just my wife! At times she can be one-sided and don't even consider what I have to say. It's like it's her way or no way!

She Say-*self talk*

Stand clear of assumptions. You know the chances of a lie but give him the benefit of the doubt!
Hold on to conclusions. This may end good. (Yea right)
Unfold those arms honey, body language is everything!
Turn down for what? Because you're loud! Let him speak and stop interrupting.

Understand the misunderstanding. Evaluate the gray areas in his dialogue.
Pretend to "get it". Nod your head and say "Mmm hmmm. Right...right."
And LISTEN! Even if you only hear 'Blah blah blah'.

Well, maybe that's just for me. I guess I can admit that I'm quick to assume he's lying, jump to conclusions, have poor body language to show lack of interest, get loud and interrupt him, and insult what he's saying by telling him it doesn't make sense.

That was a basic, humorous rundown of many conversations we've had. Over the years, I've learned that my catty ways while communicating gets me nowhere with him. Rome doesn't feed into my insults and sarcasm. He keeps me grounded by being neutral in a conversation. I'll go more into details during the chapter titled, 'Dirty Debate' where it gets a little bit deeper.

We took it upon a well know acronym expert to define or elaborate more on **Essential Factors for an Effective Conversation**. Minister Rosezina Campbell is the author of the book of spiritual acronyms, "Gifts Make Room: **G**od's **I**nsight **F**ulfilling **t**he **S**oul". To our surprise, she kept it short, sweet and simple. She said to '***LISTEN***':

Learn to
Include,
Support,
Teach,
Empower &
Nurture

She said that the most effective communicators know how to hear, what to hear, when to hear, why they hear, who to hear but most importantly, they take time to listen to understand what they are hearing.

When this acronym was conveyed to Romaro and myself, we took our time to break it down to understand and interpret what it meant to include, support, teach, empower and nurture.

We've concluded that when communicating, it's extremely important to be open-minded, supportive of one another views, and to sincerely care about the opinions and aspect of one another. Clearly, based on our acronyms, we weren't in tune with listening to one another because we already had our opinions about the conversation.

The most essential time when effective communication is vital in a marriage, is during a disagreement or argument. Get your no. 2 pencil and highlighter ready as you peruse on to the next chapter, dirty debate.

DIRTY DEBATE

HE SAY

An argument, later explained as a dirty debate by my wife, is two different opinions conflicting over one subject. The goal should always be; a mutual agreement. However, this doesn't happen often because most of the time, we have the concept that what we say is right and that the other person is wrong.

This goes into the process of perception. Perception is the way that we perceive, view or interpret things or a situation. The way you see things may not necessarily be the way that I see them. And vice versa. Having a different outlook or perception on something brings forth a debate.

In an argument, we (we as in humans in general) go as far as trying to prove the other person wrong by reducing their credibility and tearing down their views with degrading comments or remarks. These types of occurrences simply result in a debate turned into an argument which could escalate to highly expressing anger or even a physical confrontation.

Now, before I continue, let's make it clear that I have never and will never physically put my hands on my wife. But on the other hand, she's allowed her anger to dictate her actions by acting over aggressively during an argument.

Before I allow her to have her mini temper tantrums, I like to take control of our arguments. My tactic to deescalate the situation, for starters, is to simply listen to what she has to say. Half the time, she has a lot to say, on and off topic. The things she says are usually one sided and not to the point.

See, most women love to talk. Don't for one second think I'm being biased towards women. This is a general statement and opinion of mine. I'm entitled to that.

Women love to hear themselves talks. In an argument, I listen to what she has to say. If I interrupt or listen to response versus listen to understand, it upsets her that concerns are being ignored.

I understand where she comes from when she says that I'm not listening to her. Women, or at the least my wife, are emotional and no matter how small or big a conflict is, to them, it means the world is about to end.

Men tend to overlook a woman's emotions by categorizing things as unimportant based on the "size" of the situation. It goes back to perception, we look at them from our viewpoint.

One of the most catastrophic 'Dirty Debates', and I mean it literally this time, is the debate between husband and wife, boyfriend and girlfriend, about the toilet seat. Fellas, it's natural for us to use the restroom without putting the toilet seat down once we're finished.

My entire life I've heard women blow up over something so small. Really? A toilet seat? A woman, child and even a toddler can effortlessly put a toilet seat back down in less than one second. Why should it be a problem? Again, it takes little to no effort, it's a rapid movement that causes no hurt, pain or agony to the person letting the toilet seat down.

The same goes for putting a trash bag into the trash can when we (men) take the garbage out. A trash bag such as Glad, is as light as a few feathers. The heavy duty Hefty brand bags are just a few ounces in weight. You simply grab the bag out the cabinet, you may have to unravel it from the roll of bags, peel it open and give it a few shakes.

To install a trash bag depends on the type of trash bin you have. You may have to tuck and tie it to secure it in place. I'll admit, putting a trash bag in the trash bin takes a bit more effort than letting a toilet seat down.

These two simple tasks create chaos in a household. They cause arguments and in the eyes of a man, a pointless, meaningless argument. Women nag about the smallest things!

Why? It's not that they don't have the strength to do it. It's because women feel that we should do these effortless duties ourselves since we're the ones that created the need for it to be done.

For me to alleviate the need for such petty arguments, I've reminded myself to *ALWAYS* let the toilet seat down when I'm done using the restroom. When taking out the trash, I simply set the trash on the side of the can once I remove it, grab a fresh trash bag, and put it in the trash bin before taking the old bag to the garbage can outside.

> *"Fellas, if it's worth her addressing a matter to you, then it's worth getting the matter resolved to her." –Rome*

Do your wife a favor and break a simple bad habit or two. Learn what her pet peeves are and try to avoid them.

Experts say that it takes about 21 days to break a bad habit. For me, it took less than that. I had my mother, I mean my wife, monitor my behavior for about a week by reminding me to put the toilet seat down. Before I could even turn the water on to wash my hands, I would hear her loud, screechy voice eager to prompt me to put the toilet seat down.

It was easy after about a few days of being in the house with her. About the 4th day I told her I didn't need to be reminded any more. She stopped screaming to remind me, but she'd just go and poke her head in the bathroom when I was done to make sure I didn't forget.

It was an amusing process to go through and once I got into the habit of doing it without a doubt, I realized how simple and satisfying it was to please her by such a small gesture.

I challenge all the fellas who leave the toilet seat up, to allow your wife to nag you about it as a reminder so you can get into the habit of doing it yourself. They say if we don't do it, then they'll fall into the toilet in the middle of the night when they use the restroom.

Despite me believing that their bottom skin comes in contact with toilet water is a myth, let's end this argument once and for all. Same with the trash bag, let her bickering not bother you but remind you so you can break this minor "bad habit".

"Happy wife, happy life! The little things make a big difference." - Rome

SHE SAY

Let's start off my giving Rome a round of applause. He definitely deserves it for initiating the toilet seat and garbage bag challenge. Despite the sarcasm, the things he said regarding 'Dirty Debate' may be useful in your marriage as it is in ours.

My pastor, Pastor Rodney Campbell once told me, an argument between husband and wife should be nothing more than a 'Dirty Debate'. When this was first conveyed to me, I did a bit of digging to get a deeper meaning behind it.

An argument is:
1. An exchange of diverging or opposite views, typically a heated or angry one; and
2. A reason or set of reasons given with the aim of persuading others that an action or idea is right or wrong.

Although both definitions are self-explanatory, let's take a look at the second one. You'll see that the general idea behind an argument is to persuade the other individual that an idea or action is right or wrong. Well what happens when the person is firm with their opinion and views? What if the way you view things are senseless or meaningless to them?

Those are times when man (human beings not just men) can feel insulted. Usually when one feels insulted, they get hostile. When we get hostile, we're upset, and we say things out of anger that cannot be taken back.

So why bother arguing with someone you love? Someone you desire to spend the rest of your life with? Or better yet, your better half. If it leads into something ugly, I don't want parts!

Now, a debate on the other hand, is a formal discussion on a topic in which opposing arguments are put forward. There does not have to be hostility or insulting words in a debate.

If there is a mutual understanding of respect towards one another views, whether you agree, there should never me an argument in a relationship, simply a dirty debate of indifferences being brought to the forefront.

When conversing with a man, women, we know, most things are *NOT* up for debate! Unfortunately, when arguing with them, they seem to never comprehend our reasoning, insight or what we say no matter how many examples or scenarios we provide them.

However, studies show that most neural connections run between from the front and back parts of the same brain hemisphere in men. This could account for enhanced spatial (3-D, 4-D or hands on) and motor (muscle) control.

In women, connections run side to side across the left and right hemisphere of the brain. Studies believe this could account for women to have better verbal skills and intuitive (perception) abilities.

Basically, men typically don't have the conversational skills that we have. Man and woman can have two different cognitive levels regardless of what type of evidence is present in a debate. The thought process can still be completely different.

Ladies, remember it's a 'brain thang', you are not the crazy, delusional, insecure, over-thinker (wait yes, we are the over-thinker) or psycho wife or woman they try to make us out to be in an argument! Well, to a certain degree, we aren't.

Men will have us believing that we love arguments but, we just like order and structure. We desire for things to be logical and to make sense. In a debate, we can't always get our point across and it's frustrating. But, now, you know that you can't solely blame the man, let's blame the brain.
Now ladies, let's pump our breaks. We can be some extremely opinionated women. I can bet that some woman was reading that, excited to use it against her husband or significant other. Fine. If you do, just don't insult him or his intelligence.

Nurture it and tell him he's not at fault. Help him cope with the fact that his brain operations aren't the same as yours.

Ok I'm just kidding, it's not that deep so please don't make it that deep. We'd hate to cause conflict between two people based on this topic. No need to use this information against the other person. Just use it as a personal guide to cease the idea of always needing him to see things "your way".

PRIORITIZING

HE SAY

From a man's prospective, satisfying obligation and overall necessities at home should be the most important factor when prioritizing in a relationship and/or a marriage. Men have been naturally, the providers of the household.

The bibles say in 1 Timothy 5:8 *"But if anyone does not provide for his own, and especially for those of his household, he has denied the faith and is worse than an unbeliever."*

As the head of the house, it is essential to make sure home is taken care of before satisfying any external matters. If these things don't have any significant importance in fortifying the household, they should not be a top priority.

Priorities sometimes get confused with our wants and desires. When you focus on your wants and desires, there's a greater chance that they'll be fulfilled first, and the important things follow suit.

Please allow me to explain this in layman's terms. Say for instance, you have a married, family man that frequently works long hours in the day. At night, his wife expects him to be home and spend time with her and the family.

On the other hand, he feels that he has no social life and all he does is work and "sit in the house". When he decides to spend time with his guys, homies, bros or whatever you want to call them, she may feel neglected and in turn, state that his priorities are out of order.

This is where balancing priorities come in. Yes, the guy in the scenario above needs a break from the things he's obligated to do, yet he still has a commitment with his wife in which her needs should be considered before external desires.

The biggest key to balancing is to compromise. Now to compromise means to accept standards that are lower than desirable. In easier terms, it means to meet her half way.

Maybe instead of leaving home to hang out, a friend or two can visit the house and have a drink. Or maybe, they can arrange a double date with his friend(s) along with their mates. Compromising to satisfy the wife and still fulfill his desires would lighten the thought of her believing priorities are out of order.

Now, I'm not saying that a husband or wife shouldn't hang out, party, or do whatever without one another; but the reality of it is, satisfying home should come first. So, if the wife feels as though she should be entitled to your spare time, that's her opinion and it should be respected and enacted on.

However, time spent apart can be crucial to missing one another. Some people feel crowded and smothered when they're together all the time. Me personally, when I'm away from my wife it makes me miss her even more! As cliché as it sounds, it's my truth.

In a marriage or relationship, it is vital to balance out time for one another. At no time should a spouse feel like they are not getting the attention he/she deserves or feel second to anyone or anything else.

Men, discuss with your wife how she feels about the way you

prioritize. Communicate with one another on things that are acceptable, unacceptable and ways to balance all the things in your life out to appease you both.

Another manner of having priorities in order is financially. Every couple or household run their households different.

In old times, the man was the financial provider and worked while the wife stayed home and took care of the house and kids.

Now it's common for women to be actively employed, working in an assortment of positions be it hard labor, administrative, corporate, etc. Women now have the equality, to a certain degree, to make her own money and in some cases, may even be the breadwinner in the household.

Do the women being the breadwinner make the man any less of a man? No, it does not. Neither should it take away his position as the leader of the house. If he's a guy that refuses to work and allow you to financially take care of him, then you have a problem. You should evaluate the qualities of a man that's set out to lead a household.

This is where gender roles kick in. There are some things that, in my opinion, a man should not accept. If the wife is the breadwinner or makes more than you but you still work hard and bring money to the table, that doesn't make you any less of a man.

I'll say this nicely... If you're a man, and you're in between jobs, or have barriers blocking you from gaining employment while your wife brings home the bacon, you have a different type of role to fulfill. Yes, it's a tough situation because I've been there. Just hang on!

In hanging on, take care of the house in other aspects. Make sure your working wife comes home to a clean house. Give her a break from the kid(s), if any, when she comes home. Run any errands she may have while she's at work. Prepare dinner for her. If you can't cook, learn how to cook!

Just don't become complacent and allow her to work hard and be the sole provider of the house. Have your priorities in check and make sure you are making effort to become employable. Learn a trade, get a specific license, volunteer, do something!

On the financial tip, there's also a matter of prioritizing based on the way you spend it. Whether it's a one (man or woman) income household or a two-income household with either one the breadwinner, there should always be a common ground on how finances are spent.

Some men take care of all the financial needs whether the wife works or not. Some couples split bills 50/50 and keep their finances separated. Others like my wife and I, we share finances.

The way our house operates is less confusing and has never been an issue the entire ten years we've been together. We have shared finances and shared bank accounts.

Someone once said to my wife that all wives should have a hidden bank account in case we go through with a divorce. As "smart" as the advice sounds, it's a silly concept when marriage is til' death. It's like taking birth control pills while trying to get pregnant. Wow!

When she gets my paycheck, she takes care of "the bills". I added the quotation marks because I personally don't monitor what she's paying and how much she's paying. Being a financially responsible person, I know important things will get taken care of.

Once the house is in order, we make sure the kids and their necessities are in order. Once they're out the way, we use what we want for our personal use on an individual level yet we're mindful that we are a part of a household and don't take spending overboard.

Besides my wife's couponing and clearance shopping habit, I don't have too many issues with her splurging because I know she saves money in other areas, so she deserves to treat herself.

On the flip side, I am bit of a high maintenance guy. Some things, okay most things, are pretty pricey. Before spending lump sums of money on things I desire, I consult with my wife. Don't get it twisted, I do not ask her for permission; I consult with her for the simple fact that we try to keep open communication about where our hard-earned funds are allocated.

SHE SAY

Prioritize means to determine the order for dealing with a series of items or tasks according to their relative importance. It can be difficult for a woman to prioritize, on one accord, with a man. For me, even more with an older, or as he like to say, with a more experienced man.

With my experienced husband, he already knows everything. He knows what should be done before it's even needed to be done. He flat out does what he feels should be done in his own matter, way and sometimes, without even consulting me about it.

Not that he does incorrect or unacceptable things, it's all about his timing. He tends to do the wrong things at the wrong time. Being the grown man that he is, he just does what he wants to do. Of course ladies, that's *ONLY* my husband that prioritize the way I mentioned above. (Yea right! Lol)

Women, we put things in chronological order, breaking down

each segment in detail with full reasoning why things are placed in such an order. Some men (*perhaps most, perhaps all*) have no rationale behind the vast majority of the things they do.

In our marriage, we like to lay down the platform of what is most important for our household prior to putting forth our own needs, wants and desires. Whether it's time, attention or money, we make sure the house and the kids are first in line.

Prioritizing, as well as numerous topics in this book, revolves around communication in a marriage. I cannot emphasize enough how marvelous things can be if communication is on point and priorities are in order.

When priorities are not the same or cause havoc due to difference, this is when discrepancies ought to be discussed and a common resolution needs to be negotiated.

If home is lacking affection, direction, connection or necessity, one should truly rethink the situation. There was a seasonal mechanism that we experienced in which my top priorities were elsewhere and my home and everyone in it, received very little attention from me.

Marriage is a seasonal mechanism. Seasonal is fluctuating or restricted according to the season or time of year. A mechanism is a natural or established process by which something takes place or is brought about. When the seasons change as it relates to weather, there's a variation or adjustment that must take place.

Before summer enters in full bloom, the temperature slowly warms up with spring. As summer exits, it cools down with autumn. It doesn't just go from summer to winter, there's an adjustment that takes place in between.

Sometimes in life and in a relationship or marriage, we become complacent in a season. When the season change, at times, we may not agree with it or as a matter of fact, we may not even know how to handle the changes.

Recently we've encountered a season in which my priorities were modified. It's like the weather went from bright and sunny to freezing cold with snowstorms. I wasn't prepared for the new weather, so I didn't know how to adjust accordingly.

My grandmother was diagnosed with Stage IV cancer and it took my focus off my everyday life and placed it on her in the beginning of 2017. I needed to be in her presence as much as I could. I'd work long shifts then sit with her until sunset.

My mood was often shallow and I felt myself slipping in an unfamiliar place. My husband was extremely supportive, and I must say, he helped me keep my sanity. He'd pray for and with me daily and encourage me to be around my family to bond during such a trying time.

When I lost my granny May 17th, 2017, my whole world came crashing down. I began losing myself emotionally, physically and mentally. I struggled with day to day activities from getting out of bed, doing every day household duties and worst of all, being a mother to my kids and a wife to my husband.

Yet during this season, I'd often acknowledge my short comings of my priorities at home and express my desire to do better. I'd set short term goals for things that use to be second nature. Things as small as, "I'll clean the kitchen 'for real' today," yet in the pass, there was rarely an unclean kitchen.

I found myself apologizing for not having my priorities in check. But Rome never complained, pointed a finger or criticized me. He was understanding, nurturing and tolerant in the areas where I lacked. This season became a depressing season for me. A season of uncertainties and insecurities while I picked up the pieces to try and find myself!

I struggled for months trying to figure out if I was still fit to be the wife that I once was. Time and time again I'd attempt to push away from him and hide myself in shame. Again, he never complained or criticized me.

Our normal 50/50 became a 30/70 with me giving less than I ever had before. The chemistry between us altered. Rome had transitioned gracefully into this season. He hugged me tighter at night, he kissed me longer during passionate moments and he loved on me like never before!

I struggled with rapid weight gain and he embraced it! He admired the changes and reassured me that I was still his beautiful Queen. He accepted my downfalls and picked up my slack. He never showed a judgmental side or discredited me for the things I didn't do. During this season, my husband remained true to our vows.

"For better or for worse."

I never sought out any professional counseling for my fall into depression. My counseling was my praise. I praised God longer and harder because I knew that He had the power to give me back the piece of sanity I was missing. He had the power to restore my strength during my weak moments.

Without that relationship with God in our marriage, this could have been a season of Rome belittling me for not having my priorities in order. He could have wandered off for "proper" sexual satisfaction because I wasn't there. But he didn't.

It was an experience that had to happen. A change in season and priorities that didn't bring forth sunshine and beautiful blue skies. However, it was a season of understanding and empathizing. He knew all along, this too shall pass, and my priorities would eventually get back on track.

STEP PARENTING

WE SAY

When you enter a relationship, whether you know if there will be longevity or not, if you have a child(ren), always keep in mind that the individual, male or female comes with a package deal. It's a combo without *a la carte*! You can't have one and not the other.

Most people, primarily women, would suggest that they get to know a person on an individual basis before bringing them around the child(ren).

We slightly disagree with this customary idea. We believe that the child(ren) should be a part of the "getting to know you" phase in a relationship. Once you get to the point that there could potentially be an open relationship, the child(ren) should be interactive to a certain extent.

Not saying every time the two of you are together or go out, the child(ren) should be present but it would be a waste of time to get to know one another on a personal level just for the person not be "compatible" with your children.

It is a selfish act to exclude the importance of the child(ren) to be around a person that could possibly play a major role in their lives. Don't get the idea that the child has say-so on who to date or not, but not every guy or girl has the ability to adapt and nurture a child(ren) that is not biologically theirs.

A close female friend of ours dated a guy for several months. He was the perfect gentlemen, financially stable, and the two were inseparable! They talked all the time about their future and had plans on moving their relationship to the next level.

He had no children and she a toddler. He'd see pictures of him, hear all about him and even talk to him on the phone. She waited until she thought he was a good fit for her before bringing him around her child.

When she finally introduced him, he got along well with him. He played games with him, interacted with him when around and she saw great characteristics that would assume he'd make a great father figure to her son.

As time went on, maybe a few weeks to a month, the red flags flew up. He began to show signs of jealousy and selfishness. He frequently wanted to exclude her child from their outings. He'd get upset when she brought him around at times which caused a lot of chaos. She had to break it off because he became overly possessive of her.

She wasted many months getting to know this guy, who simply wanted her to himself. If she had considered bringing him around her child periodically during the "getting to know you" phase, she may have detected it early on that he was not the one for her.

This is by no means an excuse to bring multiple men/women around your kids. It's merely a notion to protect your child and your feelings from something that appears to be present but in actually, is nonexistent.

There are other factors less than and greater than the overly possessive factor which could determine if someone would be suitable to fulfill the shoes of a step-parent.

Now on the flip side of things, let's dig deeper into an established relationship or even a marriage.

HE SAY

As we revealed during the History chapter in this book, Clarissa's first-born son, Davonte, is not my son biologically. This has to be one of the first occasions in which I expressed this situation and quite frankly, it seems like I'm being dishonest when I say that he isn't my son.

I'm sure it may have "fooled" some of you, many aren't aware of this but again, we wanted to be transparent and truthful in this book. But there should not be a visible line between parenting and "step-parenting".

In the past, I've been with women that had other children. They always looked up to me because I've always been a nurturer and if they were in the household, they were treated as if they were my children.

I can remember when Clarissa was still pregnant with Davonte. There was a bond that I didn't get a chance to have with all my children prior to him.

When you live a certain lifestyle of the world and in the streets, you're not always there for your family the way that you ought to be.

This is where I'd like to be transparent. There were years of absence in some of my children lives. Sometimes it was my decision to be absent and others it was their mothers due to the hurt, pain, neglect and heartbreak that I may have inflicted on them.

These are things that men should take in consideration. The life you live, whether you admit it or not, has an impact on your children and their futures. Prison by no means was my goal but it was my consequence.

When my objective was tainted, so was my mission and vision in life. Now that it has changed, I still must reap the consequences from those actions.

Back to step-parenting. While Clarissa was pregnant, I got to experience some of the things I missed with some of my own children. It created a bond between Davonte and I in which I have never considered him to even be my stepson.

I've been around him his entire life, all nine years and I've never treated him less than the other two children I have with Clarissa.

As the man of the house, I'm to lead and set an example of what a man in the household should look like. I'd be a fool to partially parent the children at home by not parenting the one that is not mine biologically.

SHE SAY

When Rome and I got together, I accepted the fact that he had other children. To be honest, I come from a father with many kids from multiple women. Some things just seemed to be "normal".

My mother has been with my stepfather since I was three years old. Despite always being that father figure in my life, I still considered him to be a stepfather. He's always been a **step**father in my eyes because my biological father never stepped away.

My father's previous wife was in my life about the same length of time, since about age three. However, she wasn't the most pleasant to live with and be around growing up. As kids, we would often refer to her as Lady Tremaine from Cinderella.

But we weren't always the best of kids. My sisters and I were trouble makers and fire starters. The things she's done and said over the years cannot be justified or excused. There were some unacceptable behaviors in which set a precedent to the things I know not to do as a stepmother.

There can be many obstacles, challenges, boundaries and limits to what a step-parent does. The greatest challenge that I face being a stepmother is the age difference.

All the mothers of his kids are old enough to be my mother. The respect that I was his girlfriend, eventually became his wife, wasn't and to some to this day, isn't there. It's not so much of the matter of them disrespecting me, it's the level of respect that their children (young adults) aren't required to give me. If that makes sense.

My maturity level cannot be measured by my age. I've been labelled an "old soul" my entire life. But this doesn't go for people that don't know you or never took the time to get to know you.

One thing that we lacked from the beginning is that relationship we talked about that should be present with the kids and the nonparent during the "get to you stage". Of his six children, only three were around regularly since day one.

The others had a personal preference not to be around their dad for isolated reasons. This goes back to the type of character he had prior to giving his life to God. Although it was not acceptable, it's the root behind the decision some of his children to be distanced.

For the ones that were present since the beginning, two of them less than five years younger than I am. I never expected to be that "mother figure" in their lives because not only were their mothers present but it's not a comfortable feeling on either end. That's just how it is.

For his youngest, Shala, everyone knows that she is my daughter!! We've had an unbreakable bond since she was four years old when we got together.

She's never been treated like a stepchild even though she lives outside the household. My siblings, my mother and my family treat her as if she's one of my children. Same for friends, family and our church members- everyone knows that she's my baby.

But even with her, there have been limits set by her mother. Her mother is the woman that Rome continued to go back and forth with at the beginning of our relationship. So, there has been some rival-like moments throughout the years.

Shala is not a misbehaved child, so I've never really had to discipline her. If she does anything out of line, I correct her. We've never had any matters in which her mother addressed me or Rome stating that I've crossed the line as a "step" mother.

Shala and I had the opportunity to gain a relationship from start. Even though it didn't happen with the others, I often reach out and interact with my adult stepchildren. As a parent and in my case a step-parent, you just don't turn your back on them even when they don't want to be bothered. You just place limits on what you do based on what they allow and keep the doors open for improvement.

I once read that, *"A step-parent is so much more than just a parent! They made the choice to love when they did not have to!"* Whether it's loving on the inside or loving from the outside, the love is there. But the actions behind it aren't always at arm reach.

LOVE

HE SAY

What I'm about to say now just might throw some of my readers through a loop. But if you hang on tight until the end, I promise I'll bring you back around the loop to the beginning for a complete understanding. This is a preacher's mentality, some of you may already know that's how it goes.

The word love has always and will continue to be used out of context. It's precise meaning has been overlooked and undermined to the sense where we've become content and receptive to its verbiage even when it doesn't justly exist.

In doing so, we get into intimate relationships then we marry the individual without even loving them. We often say we love the person and impose that "in our hearts", we truly love that person.

Well, after talking with God on the true meaning and concept of love as it relates to marriage, He told me that love comes after marriage. I'll repeat that just to certify that you did not read a typo or misprint. I'll even isolate my statement for clarity.

"Love comes AFTER marriage." -Rome

Passion and *lust* are often confused and misinterpreted as love. As you all may have noticed, my wife and I are fond of providing definitions when we mention certain words. Words have various definitions and meanings. We like to provide clarity over a term when getting a point across.

Passion is defined as a strong and barely controllable emotion. An emotion is a natural instinctive state of mind deriving from one's circumstance, **mood,** or relationship with others. The word mood stands out in the definition of emotion. A mood is subject to change. Remember that, a mood is subject to change.

Now, lust on the other hand is having a very strong sexual desire for someone. When two have sexual intercourse out of wedlock, they experience an immense passion for one another based on the emotions or mood experienced which ultimately trailblazes to lust.

Don't get me wrong, not all married individuals experienced sexual intercourse before marriage, some remained pure until marriage. In their situation, they experienced passion prior to marriage.

The bible tells us in 1 Corinthians 7:8-9 *"To the unmarried and the widows I say that it is good for them to remain single, as I am. But if they cannot exercise self-control, they should marry. For it is better to marry than to burn with passion."*

When two people marry, it's because they have chemistry; a special connection between them that is desirable, and it feels good. To avoid burning with passion and lust, you make that vow and become one. So again, I say, two people get married out of lust and the passion they share amongst one another.

Once married, this is where **love** comes in. But you must marry someone to learn how to love them. My wife will explain, in detail, the different types of love during the 'She Say' segment. I'll soon be bringing clarity to those that may still be in that loop.

The bible tells us in Ephesians 5:21-25 *"Submit to one another out of reverence for Christ. Wives, submit yourselves to your own husbands as you do to the Lord. For the husband is the head of the wife as Christ is the head of the church, his body, of which he is the Savior. Now as the church submits to Christ, so also wives should submit to their husband in everything. Husbands, love your wives, just as Christ loved the church and gave himself up for her."*

For my saved readers, how much did you love God before you accepted Him into your life as your Lord and Savior? Think about when you first got saved. You changed your ways out of the love you have for Him. But it wasn't until the covenant with Him, that personal relationship, that you learned to love God by your actions.

The same thing happens once you get married. When you submit to one another, you submit or obey out of love and out of reverence to your marriage. It wasn't until your union was completed that you honored your wife or husband and became submissive, loyal, and that action of **love** truly came about.

"I love you," is something we should say regularly to our spouses out of assurance that we'll act upon it. Whether it's when you depart, when you're apart, or even when you greet, it continues to enhance the chemistry as well. It's used in vain when the actions aren't lined up behind the verbiage.

A good friend of mine once said,
  "When chemistry is gone, the history doesn't matter."
  -Lewis Stokes

This is accurate in relation to any intimate relationship and marriage. Chemistry keeps the attraction and special connection intact. It helps the love continue to grow and prevents it from fading away. Marriage is an eternal unification, until death do us part. In order to love, there must be chemistry and fire blazing at all times.

Love is beyond an emotion. When you love someone, you love them despite your **mood** or the circumstance you're up against.

SHE SAY

The Ancient Greeks came up with four terms to embody the emotion, or action that we often refer to as, love. Those four types of love are Agape, Phileo, Storge, and Eros.

The first of the four is Agape which means unconditional love. This is a love that exist regardless of changing circumstances. It's often referred to as 'The love of God'.

Phileo means friend bond. This is a love that exist between friends as close as siblings in strength and duration. It's a strong bond that exist to people who share common values, interests and activities. It is more of a brotherly love.

Storge or familial bond is the natural and instinctual affection as in the love a child has for its parent and vice versa.

Eros is the erotic bond. This is the passionate, intense love that arouses romantic feelings. Of all the loves, one would think that in a relationship or marriage, the love that's superior above the others would be the Eros love. As important as an erotic bond is and should be in a relationship, it should not come before Agape, Phileo or Storge.

Think about each type of love and their meanings. Grasp your own interpretation of each one. You should easily be able to place the people in your life in a category based on the type of love you have for them.

In my opinion, your spouse should sustain a status in each category. They all go hand in hand. A spouse cannot be in one category without being in the others.

The Agape love supersedes them all. Despite the dilemmas in a marriage, you must love your spouse unconditionally. Regardless what obstacles or differences come up, that Agape love you have for them doesn't and shouldn't change. If you can love your spouse any less due to a circumstance, then there is a serious doubt in whether or not the love is genuine.

My husband is *not* my best friend. I have several female friends that I consider to be my best friends. There are things that I feel comfortable discussing with them that I cannot discuss with him. My best friends and I have interest in things that my husband and I don't share.

Does that not make him my friend? No, it doesn't. He's an excellent listener, he's cool to hang around, we share secrets and make lots of memories together. We support one another in all our endeavors, but it's a completely different level of friendship. But we do have a Phileo bond.

Same with Storge love. He's not my child and he's not parent. Despite being the same age as my parents…. "OMG!! Did I just read that?" I'm sure you questioned yourself. You sure did! The cat is out the bag. Rome is the same age as my parents.

Sidebar: *Love has no age limit! Our twenty year (nineteen years and eleven months to be exact) difference has never been a barrier to us or the love we have for one another. My parents were approving from the jump, with slight warnings, but they did offer their blessings for me to proceed with being in a relationship with him.*

Continuing, in a marriage you share the Storge type of love because you are equal, you're one. The Storge love, once again is that natural, instinctual affection so it's bound to be present.

Genesis 2:22-24 reads, "*Then the Lord God made a woman from the rib he had taken out of the man, and he brought her to the man. The man said, 'This is now bone of my bones and flesh of my flesh; she shall be called 'woman' for she was taken out of man.*

That is why a man leaves his father and mother and is united to his wife, and they become one flesh."

The final love, Eros is that sexual bond. It's that romantic and passionate type of love that usually comes with an implication of sexual deeds.

When sharing passionate moments together, you are *one* as it is with Storge love, experiencing Phileo due to creating *memories* and Agape because all *differences are set aside* when Eros love is in action.

LOVEMAKING

WE SAY

What better way to proceed after discussing Eros love than to talk about lovemaking? Yes, I know, we couldn't think of a could we think of a better either. When we hear sexual bond, as a married couple, we think about lovemaking!

Hebrews 13: 4 says, *"Let marriage be held in honor among all, and let the marriage bed be undefiled, for God will judge the sexually immoral adulterer."*

Undefiled is another word for pure. So, purity is what God ordained in the bedroom. We won't elaborate on this but let each man examine himself and his marriage alone. We are not the ones to cast judgement.

The book of Corinthians has quite a few scriptures on sex in a marriage. 1 Corinthians 7:5 says, *"Do not deprive one another, except perhaps by agreement for a limited time, that you may devote yourselves to prayer, but then come together again, so that Satan may not tempt you due to your lack of self-control."*

There are at least five more scriptures that's like 1 Corinthians 7:5. When we realized this several years ago, we understood that there must be some intense importance behind it.

Depriving one another from sex, as it states in the bible, can lead to temptation; due to the lack of self-control one may have those sexual desires fulfilled elsewhere.

The key factor we personally would like to encourage all married couples to do in the bedroom is to _communicate_. In all areas of marriage, communication is vital.

Discuss, in details, do's and don'ts of the bedroom. Converse about what satisfies you and what turns you off. Although these topics appear to be ordinary things one should know about their spouse in the bedroom, unfortunately they are not.

I, Clarissa, was a Pure Romance Consultant for about four years. As a consultant, many customers would come to me for advice and assistance with communicating with their spouse or significant other. There'd be things that their spouse does that they didn't like yet they pretend to like.

Whether you're like most men who like to have sex or like most women who like to experience romance, the ultimate outcome of the lovemaking experience is an orgasm or climax. Yes, the magical moments primary to climax is amazing but, in all honesty, the climax is the goal.

You wouldn't believe the statistics of women who 1) Have never experienced an orgasm and 2) Fake orgasms on a regular basis. This is not up for debate, as crazy as it sounds, it's factual information, not opinions.

Even in marriages, many hold back their truths in the bedroom. They hold back their opinions and desires about their sex life from their spouse because they are embarrassed or don't want to be offensive. The primary disadvantage resulting from not being able to communicate, is depriving a spouse sex.

Before depriving one another to sex, it's important to resolve any issues that may be in the way. What may be a valid reason to say "no" may not be valid to the spouse that's being denied.

One of the common reasons women withdraw from the desire to make love or have sex is due to low libido or sexual desire. For women, there is a wide range of causes for decreased sex drive which includes but not limited to:

- *Physical causes*- sexual issues, medical issues, medications, birth control, drug and alcohol use, weight issues, age, and fatigue;
- *Hormonal causes*- pregnancy, breastfeeding, menopause, and low testosterone;
- *Psychological causes*- anxiety, stress, and mental illness;
- *Relationship issues*- lack of connection with your spouse (including not being able to climax), infidelity, loss of interest, history of sexual abuse, and lack of communication of sexual preferences.

However, women often use the customary excuse, "I don't feel like it". From a man's standpoint, "I don't feel like it" may not be a valid excuse to deny him sex. But what if he knew the exact causes of her low libido? Would he be more lenient, understanding and receptive to her saying no?

Maybe it's the wife. Maybe this low libido talk is new to her. Not all women know and understand their body like they think they do.

If a wife is experiencing low sex drive, there is something that can be done about it. There is sex therapy, yoga, and even Viagra. There are countless propositions that can be provided by a health care physician for specific causes on a case by case scenario.

Men on the other hand, are not all like jack rabbits as often referred as. They can also have changes in sexual desire due to low testosterone levels, health issues, age, loss of interest and more. As stated with the woman, medical consultation is recommended for more accurate diagnosis and treatments.

The second important bedroom factor is _respect_. Respecting one another in the bedroom brings forth comfortability which can lead to willingness to do and try different things and engaging freely.

Two of my favorite books that I'd personally like to recommend to all married couples is "*Tickle His Pickle*" and "*Tickle Your Fancy*" by Sadie Allison. There are also many erotic books to take your lovemaking to another level. I promise, you'll thank me later!

With the respect of one another, be open to try new things to keep the bedroom spicy. Keep the excitement of pleasing your significant other at all times.

The final factor in the bedroom is to swear to _secrecy_. Never share your bedroom secrets with anyone. What happens between you all, should stay between you all and is for your information only.

Why would one willingly open the door for lust to intrude? Whether you share the downfalls or the mountain tops of your sexual experiences, you risk opening the door for curious cats.

There are some "exceptions" on what can be shared. Not all people will agree with these "exceptions". Even Rome disagree with me on this.

In my opinion, exceptions would be directly or indirectly commenting on lovemaking or a sexual topic in general- without being too detailed. As a member of a secret group on Facebook specifically for wives, there are days where we have a thread of 'After Dark' talk.

I love engaging on these threads! Not only do I learn a lot to apply to my own sex life, but I have a level of expertise in the subject that has been proven to benefit other wives from advice I've given.

It is extremely important to keep the lovemaking spicy and exciting. Let's be honest here; no one really likes normal, routine sex. The bedroom in a marriage should be unpredictable as much as possible!

I know, life and little ones get in the way and sometimes, arrangements must be made just to have that intimate time and that's okay.
Of course, this should not take over the spontaneous, normal "routine" of sex, but there are couples who's daily lives interfere with giving it up every time the other spouse desires it.

Keep your spouse in amazement of the avenues you take to satisfy him or her. Wow them with your efforts of putting a smile on their face and getting them warm on the inside! My point is, spice it up sometimes!

Do different to achieve different. Some may say don't fix something that's not broken, but not broken doesn't mean it's not bent or doesn't need to be revitalized.

Theoretical Physicist Albert Einstein said, "*Insanity is doing the same thing over and over again and expecting a different result.*" Defeat insanity in the bedroom by initiating our "Spicy Detour Ideas" with your spouse.

Dare to do different, explore, spice up, and open up to new ideas and concepts! Here's a few ideas to keep things spicy! To turn it up a few notches, read the two books by Sadie Allison.

7 Day Sex Challenge
Implement a full week, 7 days long, at least one session each day, of bedroom pleasure! Give it a try and watch the vibes between you all beautifully harmonize at the eagerness to get to 7th day. Enjoy making love and magic to and with your partner!

Someone may already have the opportunity to experience it daily. However, it's not that common. We also created a week long (not the same week of the 7 Day Sex Challenge) one of these other 'Spicy Detour Ideas.'

Sexy Sunday
When you look good, you feel good! Do a date night before the week begins and get sexy! Go beyond basic beauty, get extra in your own special way. Slay for the Gods ladies! Fellas, get handsome just the way she likes it with too much sauce! Sexy and sauce to start the week!

Mating Monday
Maybe you're attempting to conceive. Make Mondays magical and make music! Mate on Mondays!

Tune-in Tuesday
Tune-in to one another sexual senses. Verbally explore each other's fantasies, desires and what's enjoyable and what's not enjoyable. Take the time to Tune-in to your spouse's truths and their preferences!

Wild Out Wednesday
Go crazy! Get spontaneous! Get wild! Remember the first two important factors in the bedroom: Communicate and respect one another. But take a day out and do something out of the extraordinary. Just Wild Out!

Throwback Thursday
Take a trip down memory lane. Think about the things that use to transpire in the bedroom that ceased. Throw em' back in there! Time changes things. Use Tune-in Tuesday as a breakthrough to initiate Throwback Thursdays. Don't forget to 'throw it back' on Throwback Thursday, it's only right!

Four-play Friday
Four-play is often abandoned in the bedroom, especially for

the wives. Men are like microwaves and women are like ovens, we take a while to heat up! Let us bake beyond the bedroom! What better way to arouse one another than to make an entire day out of four-play? Send a freaky text while at work or DM a freaky pic. Once it's time to cook, enjoy a magnitude for four-play!

Selfless Saturday
Sometimes we jump into bed with thoughts of how we'll get ourselves "off". Stop and be self-less. Take Saturday's sex and do it selflessly! Take turns making it all about one another. This is the perfect time to hit your spouses spot(s)! Stay selfless and service your loved one!

Have fun with these days. Switch them up, create your own if you think those are too corny or whatnot. Two other techniques we've incorporated in our marriage are listed below.

Deserted Phone Date
Make it a rule of thumb to have cellphone-less dates. With advance technology and the social media world today, too often has dating become less about spending quality time and more about cellular devices.

We live in a time where we 'check in' at locations now. When we're out on our casual dates (no married couple should EVER stop dating), we take a few pics, check in and put our phones away. It gives us focus on each other and it feels amazing!

Work-free Weekend
For some reason, there is always a spouse, if not both, that works around the clock. When it's a "by choice" situation and it causes concerns whether addressed or not, enjoy a work-free weekend with your mate. Give them your undivided attention and take a mental break from business and work.

To sum up lovemaking, never stop making it happen! There are numerous things that can prevent the desire to do it but do whatever it takes to make sure you keep the fire blazing. And never stop learning your significant other.

The secret to lovemaking is to create emotional openness, become one, and supply one another with physical pleasure that develops deeper as time goes on.

> *"Lovemaking... The supernatural forces are beyond lips and genitals while soaring pass the mind... It induces a climax from the soul so beautifully and divine."* -Clarissa

HOME IMPROVEMENT

My (Clarissa) newly found profession is a licensed Real Estate Agent in the state of Wisconsin. Buying or building a house is often looked upon as #MarriageGoals. I've done research on building houses as well as home improvement. To reside in a comfortable, dream home is highly desired by many couples.

What you'll read next are tools for building a new house and refurbishing an existing one. After that, there will be an analysis on carpet cleaning, a final walk through then "setting up" the home. These tools will be true steps of the physical house creation yet metaphorically considering the marriage as the house itself.

Building

There are 7 steps to summarize the house building process. The number 7 is the foundation of God's word. And for us, the year this book is released is our 7th year of marriage. 7 is also referred to as the number of completeness.

1.) *Location*- When building a house from the ground up, the first thing to do is select a location (*spouse*) and agree that this is the ground in which you will build on. You'd have to make sure that it's a secured location, one deemed fit for longevity since you are establishing it (*marriage*) from the ground up.

2) Plan: Once the location is squared away, there is usually a plan (*proposal*) of some sort, usually something spectacular to make one truly wow the idea of building on such land. A contractor or home builder is contacted to discuss the ideas. The property is sometimes surveyed (*pre-martial counseling*) to clear up misconceptions about the grounds (*compatibility*), to create the blueprint (*marriage goals*), set forth the building process (*wedding*), to remove doubt and get a second opinion.

3.) Permits: You'd be required to get licenses (*marriage license*) and permits, construction loan, and even have the property surveyed (*parents "approval"*). These legal things are traditionally held in front of a lieu of witnesses, with workers (*bridesmaids*) and subcontractors (*groomsmen*) to assist in the building process (*wedding ceremony).*

4.) Breaking Ground: The most crucial element when building a house is the foundation. The land must be cleared of any trees (*past hurt*), weeds (*prior relationships*), rocks (*trust issues*), underbrush (*doubt*) and then leveled where the house will be built. Then the footings are dug. They are filled with rebar and poured with concrete.

Let me explain what rebar is. Rebar (*faith*), short for reinforcing bar, is collectively known as reinforcing steel (*prayer*) and reinforcement steel (*fasting*). It is a steel bar or mesh of steel wires used as a tension device or reinforced concrete to strengthen and hold the concrete in compression (*hard times*). To sum it up, rebar drastically increases the tensile or flexible strength (*endurance*) of the structure of the house (*marriage*).

5.) Floor Joists: Continuing, once the foundation (*God fearing*) is set, floor joists are nailed into place and the subfloors are constructed. Lumber is then laid out on the sub floor to create frames for the walls. The strength of this lumber is vital for the home because they help support the foundation and make the floor solid enough to withstand the structure (*martial issues*) of the house.

6.) *Framing*: Once the floor joists are completed, the framing begins. This is the most satisfying part of building a house because it creates the actual form (*family unit*) of the house. Walls, windows, doors and rooms are framed, beginning with the exterior.

The exterior walls are covered with insulation (*problem solving*) and plywood (*sacrifices*). There are many different types of insulation. Some types are more effective than others and for the most part, they come with a higher cost. The purpose of insulation in a house is to create a barrier around the structure, over the roof, on the walls and beneath the floors to reduce the amount of heat entering the home on a warm day and reducing the amount of heat loss on a cold day. In other words, it makes it energy efficient (*withstand strongholds*).

7.) *Essentials*: After framing is completed, here's where the electricians (*wife*) and plumbers (*husband*) work together to install wiring for all electrical needs and plumbing work for the water supply system, drainage pipes, and sewerage system.

Once the electrical and plumbing is complete, the finishing touches are put onto the house. These include the interior finishes such as installing cabinets, panels, wallpaper, caulk, paint, carpet, tile, etc.

Refurbishing

To refurbish means to renovate and redecorate something. There is a such thing as normal wear and tear (*petty issues*) of a house. However, damage can also be done to a house from catastrophic and unforeseen events depending on what region or even the type of land a house is built.

Catastrophic disasters include, but are not limited to,

hurricanes (*infidelity*), floods, wind, tornados, tsunamis (*abuse*), and earthquakes. Unforeseen events include, but are not limited to, fires, theft, vandalism (*clashing*) or accidental damage such as water from plumbing issues (*incompatibility*).

These things may cause damage to the exterior as well as the interior and may require refurbishing (*counseling*) if it's not destroyed and a total loss (*divorce*).

To relieve the anguish of getting repairs done in the event of a disaster to your house, homeowners insurance (*God's assurance*) is highly recommended and in some cases, not an option to a homeowner.

A house (*marriage*) is likely to be one of the most valuable assets one may have. Homeowner's insurance protects the investment (*vow*). It doesn't protect it from the damage (*issues*) itself, but it may help provide a financial safety net (*covering*) should the unexpected occur.

Let's say a house (*marriage*) endured a severe storm (*emotional abuse*). The storm ripped shingles from the roof (*hurt*), uprooted (*childhood hurt*) a tree in the yard causing it to topple over onto the structure, resulting in interior damage (*low self-esteem*) as well.

With homeowner's insurance (*God's assurance*), you can submit a claim (*cry out*) to the insurance company for reimbursement (*deliverance*) to make the necessary repairs (*emotional healing*) or refurbish the damaged property (*hurt spouse*).

Maybe damage wasn't the case. Maybe the normal wear and tear (*lack of communication, decreased sex drive, financial issues*) turned into eye sores and you decided to rectify the situation by fixing it up (*resolve conflict*) or redecorating, before major damage occurs.

When it's not a house built from the ground, the condition may not be sustainable from the previous owner and refurbishing it may be needed. Some houses are inherited (*generational curses*) after the death of a parent/grandparent and the condition may not be updated or to one's liking so they may require a bit of renovating (*renewing*).

Carpet Cleaning

Colossians 3:18-19 says, "*Wives, submit yourselves to your husbands, as it is fitting in the Lord. Husbands, love your wives and do not be harsh with them.*"

To submit or be submissive means to obey and to follow. So yes, wives have been instructed to obey and follow their husbands.

With marriage being a sacred union between two in which what happens in a marriage is no one else's business, too often, things are swept "under the rug".

When a wife isn't submissive, then the man can't lead. We believe that wives are defiant on being submissive to their husbands based on several things:

1. Generational curse of a broken home in which single mothers are the head of the household with absent fathers;
2. Independent women are prevalent in today's society; and
3. Wives distrust husbands based on past experiences.

Broken home is indeed a generational curse. As children, we look to our parents as role models. For the single mother, it's favorable in a daughter's eyes to be just as strong and independent as momma was. The strength of a single mother that 'makes it happen' and makes it look easy through the struggle is appeasing to the eye.

According to the U.S. Census Bureau, out of 24 million children in America, 1 out of 3 children live without their biological father in the household. Research shows that when a child is raised without a father, children are affected in these ways:

- ❖ 2x's more likely to drop out of high school,
- ❖ 4x's greater risk of poverty,
- ❖ 7x's more likely for girls to become teen mothers,
- ❖ more likely to go to prison,
- ❖ more likely to face abuse and neglect,
- ❖ more likely to have behavioral issues,

and sadly, this list goes on and on.

There is a cycle that continues from generation to generation and from coast to coast.

It's disastrous yet common for a man, father or even a husband, to physically be in the household but the woman, mother or wife cannot depend on him to be there for her, the children and/or the household. So, the strength of a wife is second nature versus being solely submissive or reliant on the man of the house to lead.

Now, there is a broad number of reasons why men have been known not to lead or to be absent in a household. Those reasons can be based on economic, social, ethnic, cultural, and regional disadvantages and status. We will not get into details about these barriers yet one may research themselves to get a broader understanding if desired.

If there's a high percentage of males being raised in single mother households, then how can they be taught "how to be a man" and how to lead a household? This is once again, the cycle of a generational curse. How can one lead unless he is taught?

As a wife, it is difficult to be submissive in a marriage when all hell has broken loose and vice versa for a husband to lead.

Abuse is one of the most common issues that causes havoc in a marriage. Verbal, psychological, emotional, sexual and physical abuse are issues couples deal with and unfortunately, silently tolerate. When there is abuse in a marriage, it's often "swept under the rug".

Verbal abuse is a type of emotional abuse which includes yelling, degrading, belittling, blaming, accusing, cursing, nagging, embarrassing, etc. It causes emotional pain to another person. When it comes to relationships, it's often an indication that psychological and physical abuse is also present.

According to Wikipedia, psychological abuse is a form of abuse, characterized by a person subjecting, or exposing, another person to behavior that may result in psychological trauma, including anxiety, chronic depression, or post-traumatic stress disorder.

Psychological abuse is also concern of what the other spouse may think or say. That feeling of uncertainty of one's reaction can cause anxiety due to having an undecisive or uneasy feeling.

Example: *A wife was invited to a holiday party at work. She has the desire to attend but must get "permission" from her husband. She may experience anxiety prior to asking him, knowing he's short tempered and she's uncertain if she should even ask based on the fear of his response both verbally and maybe even physically.*

In a situation like that, it disregards a person's self-esteem and their ability to make decisions on their own. It also gears your mind away from your own personal thoughts, perception and gives the other person a sense of control or power over you.

> *"Control the marriage, not the spouse."*
> – Clarissa Green

What about the physical dangers in a marriage? The battered skeletons in the closet? Those sickening, heart-rending domestic violence episodes that are often swept under the rug? How does one get those things squared away and sterile?

According to National Coalition Against Domestic Violence (NCADV), here are a few statistics on domestic violence:

- 1 in 3 women and 1 in 4 men is a victim of some form of physical violence by an intimate partner during their lifetimes

- 76% of intimate partner physical violence victims are female; 24% are male

- More than 75% of women aged 18-49 who are abused were previously abused by the **same** perpetrator

- 40% of female murder victims are killed by intimate partners

Wow! Those statistics are definitely some eye sores. We've included the full fact sheet of statistics at the end of this book for personal reference if needed.

Let's get to the carpet cleaning! This may not be for all readers of this book. If not, great but still read this section. Maybe you know someone that's being abused in their relationship and can assist them with getting their carpet cleaned.

Start by looking at that rug you've been sweeping dirt under for months, years, or even decades. Examine the surface of it, the edges, ridges and crevices. Perhaps it's just a tad bit dusty. A regular vacuum can remove dirt from the surface, so a frequent visit of these matters is vital.

Now, lift it up and focus on the contents underneath. The scum, the filth, the unpleasant, and the hideous buildup. If you're like me, you may be allergic (*sensitive*) to dust mites and have an allergic reaction (*mental breakdown*) when cleaning (*resolving issues*) underneath. But, it's just a reaction, it'll clear up and get better sooner than later.

After you've examined the debris underneath the rug, start by removing the larger fragments from the rubble. The *"what happens in this house, stays in this house"* ... *"keep everyone out of my marriage"* .... *"he loves me"* ... *"I'm supposed to be submissive"*.

When a victim stays in an abusive relationship, they're usually conditioned to provide excuses for the abuser.

Maybe you provoked him or her to anger? Maybe you hit below the belt and he or she was bound to get physical? Better yet, maybe he or she getting better at controlling his temper? Wait, no "maybe", it's not as bad as it could be or even as it used to be!

Sometimes we hold excuses so dear to our heart they become troubled truths! That type of debris is the most dangerous of its kind.

Once again, the statistic above says, more than 75% of women age 18-49 who are abused was previously abused by the same perpetrator or significant other. That goes to show that if it happens once, it more than likely will happen again!

Not all private matters deserve to be covered up. Some need to be exposed and treated before they seep through the rug and cause external damage.

Any victim of physical abuse whether it be in a past relationship or a current one, knows that the abuser is usually apologetic. And after apologies, promises to change or oaths to not do it again follows.

There is absolutely no valid reason or excuse for physical abuse. It is a choice that one was willing to make and is unacceptable at all costs. Married or not, LOVE DOESN'T HURT!!

"Love is patient, love is kind. It does not envy, it does not boast, it is not proud. It does not dishonor others, it is not self-seeking, it is not EASILY ANGERED, it keeps no record of wrongs. Love does not delight in evil but rejoices with the truth. It always protects, always trusts, always hopes, always preserves." – 1 Corinthians 13:4-7.

I can guarantee, *love* is the top reason why a person stays in an unhealthy, abusive relationship. What's love got to do with it? *EVERYTHING!*

This goes back to the highest standard of the four types of love mentioned earlier in this book, Agape. That's the "Even though he/she is abusive, I still love him/her. Even though he/she don't treat me right, I still love him/her." It's unconditional which once again, means love without conditions or limitations.

When you unconditionally love someone, it's not easy to pack up and walk away. It's so much easier said, than to act on it. That's not an opinion from the Green's, but a fact.

Abuse is accepted because of love, the vows, the desire to maintain that family unit or structure, and even out of fear. The fear of being alone, being without that toxic person, fear of losing tangible things like cars, houses and other assets that provide financial security which can be split or loss during a divorce, even fear of physical violence if you leave.

One of the greatest fears, is for the children not to have that family unit. So, people stay in unhealthy relationships and marriages and sweep everything "under the rug" simply because of fear.

If you are afraid, face that fear by walking away or seeking help. We're not going to encourage everyone in an abusive, whether physical, emotional, psychological, or verbal, relationship to exit it. But we are going to motivate you to get help before it's too late!

If you're holding on to the hopes and faith that he or she will change one day, then make sure concrete work is being done. By concrete, we mean actual action is being done. Never rely on just verbal assurance because sadly, a word being a person's bond is becoming inexistent.

If he or she wants to change, they'll be willing to do anything to get better (*carpet clean*). Whether it's counseling, therapy, applying stress relieving techniques, or utilizing some of the skills such as communicating from this book.

Other techniques include praying, fasting, meditation, and seeking the face of God. What works for one person, may not work another. Find what type of cleaner works and don't work.

Abuse is a disease. A disease is a quality, habit or disposition regarded as hostile affecting a person or group of people. When a disease isn't treated, it worsens, and it potentially spreads. No parent should want their child(ren) to catch such a contagious, undesired illness like abuse.

No mother/father should want their child to be receptive or tolerant of abuse in their relationship when they get older. And no mother/father should want their child to be an abuser to their significant other when they grow up either. Exposing them to abuse in the household early own as kids, heightens the risk of abuse in their adult like.

The last form of abuse that's often swept under the rug is sexual abuse. This is a controversial discussion in marriage. As shocking as it may sound, it is believed that a man should and could receive sexual intercourse at any given time, with or without consent from his wife.

Some of you are like us, we definitely don't think that is morally just. Clarissa has the free will to refuse to have intercourse with me whether she provide valid reason or not. As a man, a husband and a human being, I cannot see myself taking it from her when she declines.

Taking it after she's said no, is rape whether she's your spouse or not! The bible says it should be discussed when a husband is deprived, it doesn't say he should take advantage of her and get it anyways. This is unjust and for any husband that feels that it's okay to take it from his wife, you my brother, need to really think about the harm you're doing, just for a few minutes of pleasure.

As we said before, we're not condoning divorce neither are we condoning anyone in an abusive relationship to accept it. We're pleading, matter of fact, we are begging that you clean from under that rug and clean it good!

We're not counselors but you can call the number below for professional help and counsel. This is a 24/7 hotline so they are ready to answer when you call! The phone number is 1800-799-SAFE (7233).

"If it's worth having then it's worth fighting for."
-Clarissa Green

Fighting for a marriage is putting forth a battle to keep it despite what hell is breaking loose. But the fight isn't against one another, it's against the adversities and against the excuses of not seeking help to overcome them.

Outside of abuse, other things that are swept under the rug in a marriage are works of the flesh.

Galatians 5:19-21 says, *"The acts of the flesh are obvious: sexual immorality, impurity and debauchery; idolatry and witchcraft; hatred, discord, jealousy, fits of rage, selfish ambition, dissensions, factions and envy; drunkenness, orgies, and the like. I warn you, as I did before, that those who live like this will not inherit the kingdom of God."*

Others include addictions such as drugs (legal and illegal), alcohol, shopping, theft, sex, pornography, and more.

Adultery is also swept under the rug. Matthew 26:41 says, *"Watch and pray so that you will not fall into temptation. The Spirit is willing, but the flesh is weak."*

Sin usually feels good to flesh but it burns to the spirit man. Which are you operating under? If you're operating in the flesh, then it wouldn't take much to fall into temptation.

When you stay "prayed up" as we call it and covered by God, you can avoid these temptations with no effort when you operate in the spirit.

The reality is, adultery does more damage than just about anything in a marriage. It causes psychological damage. Trust is loss, bonds are broken and hope for an ever-lasting marriage is torn.

> *"A cheater doesn't necessarily stop when they get caught or can no longer do it; they stop when they can no longer bear the consequences."* – Rome

When it's swept under the rug, it continues to happen, just like anything else. Address the issue of one stepping out on the other. Whether it's "justifiable" or not, it should be addressed with consequences if it continues.

Trust must be regained after infidelity. This will be done differently from all people. There is no right or wrong way to forgive someone.

One thing we can say is that if you continue a marriage after one steps out, try your hardest to allow that person a clean slate. It may have residue on it and carry an unpleasant stench but if you allowed it back in your life, it's worth cleaning it completely.

It's human nature to allow past experiences to dictate or set a precedent for us. We keep our guard up with fear that if it happened before, it just might happen again.

Forgiveness improves mental health, lower stress level, improves self-esteem and best of all, improves a relationship.

It's often said, "I forgive but I'll never forget.". That's absolutely okay! It's natural. It's common. And again, it's okay. It's never easy to forget about a wound whether it still hurts, still has a scab, left a scar or even if it's completely gone and no longer hurts or is visible.

Walk-through

In this book, we've covered a wide array of topics. It's impossible to include all martial topics because it's an enormously vast subject.

A walk-through is a tour or demonstration of an area or task. Now that we've built a house (*marriage*), refurbished one, and cleaned the carpet, we'll be doing a final walk-through of the property.

During this final walk-through we'll go from room to room and briefly speak and advise, based on our marriage, family life, goals and opinions based on that particular area. What works for us may not work for you. But it doesn't devalue our concept nonetheless.

1) **Yard**: The first thing visible in a yard is the mailbox. "The Green's" is written loud and proud on ours! The name change for me, Clarissa, was important to us and I did it immediately! It's an honor to take on the last name of my better half.

   Some wives don't change it for their own personal reasons but being a Mrs. is valuable enough to change my name.

   My maiden name is Brown. Having it hyphenated, Clarissa Brown-Green, sounds a bit crazy so I dropped the Brown and went Green- Go Green! LOL

   The edifice of the beauty of the yard is a shared responsibility. Whether it's décor or nature, cleanliness or maintenance, completing these tasks can be done by a duo to make them easier.

2) **Garage**: All couples should have something unique about them that may be cute yet corny, but it identifies *them.*

   Before pulling up at home or pulling into the garage, we honk the horn to let the other know we're home. Whoever is inside, usually flickers the lights, acknowledging that we heard the other outside.

   Rome has this thing where he shakes the keys before he puts them in the keyhole. Since the kids (now ages 2, 7 and 9) are smaller and still easy to entertain, we all fake sleep or hide when he enters.

   Rome comes in and hoovers over a "sleeping" body until they open their eyes, and everyone laughs. Or he'll search around the house and find us, one by one.

These little things mean a lot to our household. It sets us apart from others. It's only done at home, not when we go to other people house.

When we take trips or rides, Rome is usually the driver. Despite not being the logical driver and a poor navigating driver, I prefer to kick my feet up and ride. I often like to say, *"If he's riding, I'm rolling."*

3) **Dining room**- Due to the times we are living in where technology has an impact on our everyday lives, the family unit has resorted to technology dependency during supper. The dining room used to be the place where meals were eaten, and discussions were held amongst the family. Now texting is the number one means of communication and overruled that supper convo.

For holidays, families used to all go to 'Big mama's' house and enjoy one another's company. Nowadays, some families lack those traditions due to countless reasons.

Same for holidays. Create a family tradition. Our favorite is to prepare to-go containers and drive around the city passing out hot meals for Thanksgiving. It's love, charity and a tradition that hopefully our kids can pass on to their kids someday.

For Christmas, we drive to Big Mama's house in Michigan. The house is always filled with holiday décor, beautiful lights, love and laughter when we all sit together at the dining room table and enjoy a holiday feast together.

We challenge families to start eating together again.

Take advantage of the time spent with your loved ones. No television, no social media, no tablets, no phones- just good ole' food and conversation. Take this time to see how work was, what's being learned at school and engage like families are supposed to.

4) **Living room**- A double standard is a rule or principle that is unfairly applied in different ways to different people or groups.

Gender roles in a household, nowadays, are double standards. Some of those things include but are not limited to, pumping gas, getting vehicles services, cooking and cleaning, carrying groceries, heavy lifting, rearranging furniture, dusting, and more.

For the most part, Rome does every task that I do around the house when I don't get the chance to get to it, if I ask him if he could do it for me or if I'm too busy to do them. This includes cooking, cleaning, and sometimes laundry.

There are some things that prefer that I not do which includes pumping gas, car maintenance, lifting and moving heavy objects, and even carrying laundry or groceries.

Being muscular built, I have no issue with doing these things. However, Rome prefers that I "step to the side" and let him and our young boys handle it. If he like it, I love it!

> *"A strong woman can do it all by herself; but a stronger man will be right by her side, so she won't have to."*
> -Rome

As mentioned countless times in this book, communication is key! Communicate with your spouse on these types of things and come up with an agreement with what works for your household.

Every marriage will have different principles, morals, ethics and even goals. Discover the ones for your household and marriage and apply them to your everyday lives.

Rome aims to please me when it comes down to making things easier for me. The smallest things make the biggest difference. He does things like pick out my clothes, iron them, get the kids up and ready for school, drive my car to the front of the house, and more.

For me, I love to cater to my husband. On his off days, he usually gets three meals even if it means that I prepare more than one at a time.

As a wife, I ensure that he's coming home to a clean, relaxing home setting after work, a delicious hot meal and an ice cold drink to wash it down. I'm not one to barge him with issues when he comes home; I ask him how his day went and speak positively about what's going on.

We believe marriage is all about making things convenient for one another. From running my bath water, to charging by cell phone, he makes sure that something he does helps me out. From managing bills and appointments, to taking care of the kids, I get the job done!

As a married couple, there should be no 'independence'. I've always been proud to say that I have a husband that I can depend on for ANYTHING! We've never had the struggle of doing things by ourselves or with no help as some single parents, but that doesn't mean that without one another, we wouldn't be able to manage.

5) **Rec room**- Entertainment is important in a household.

The Ring

It gives the family time to socialize and enjoy one another. Due to our hectic work schedules, we've never had the opportunity to structure a "game night" in our house as many people do.

Once our schedules allow, we have the desire to utilize at least one day out of the week to have a family game night. It's productive, nurturing, builds bonds, helps with communication and intellectual skills, and creates unforgettable memories.

Board games, card games and even video games are incorporated in regular events but not routinely done. We do however have regular events that we like to attend together such as parades, fairs, amusement and water parks.

6) **Mancave**- Every man needs his own space! Whether it's to get away to watch sports, play video games, indulge in hobbies, or hang out with his male friends.

   A hard working man deserves a mancave! It gives him a place to recoup and relax after a long day of work.

   Mancaves shouldn't be designed with the idea of pushing a wife and family to the side but to solely have his personal space. Especially since women are typically the sole decorators and regulators of the house, a man deserves something to call his own.

   While we're in the mancave, let's address having "best" friends of the opposite sex. This one will be cut and dry! It's a NO for us. This is something we both agree on.

   Colleagues are a bit different. You're around the person by default and may even do lunch together and other social outings with other coworkers. Even then, there are limits!

Friends of the opposite sex, to us, leaves too much room for error. It has nothing to do with being insecure but simply securing a marriage that means more than a friendship with someone else. At the end of the day, countless people marry their "best friend". Case closed!

7) **Master bedroom-** The master bedroom is the most intimate area in a home. Not just sexually but emotionally, mentally and spiritually.

   It is the host of divine connection between two people. This is the area where and why two people take on the decision to become one.

   The master bedroom holds so much weight in who and what we become in life. It all boils down to the fact that we confide in and have faith in what our spouse transfers to our inner man.

   Pillow talk, also known as conversation before or after being intimate, is the in-depth, private conversations that should be edifying to the relationship.

   During pillow talk, you share your dreams, failures, aspirations, struggles, weaknesses, strengths, etc. with your significant other. This also gives you the opportunity to push one another to greatness and build each another up!

   Rome is my black king! Black kings have been degraded and devalued by society for so many years. Pillow talk is a dynamic approach to foster greatness and empowerment to his mental. During the time of intimate, mental and spiritual connection, it's conveyed as truthfulness.

   A man may feel low about himself in any aspect of his life but when it comes to the bedroom, his throne, it's up to the wife to impart the majestic notion to him that he's the king and nothing less!

The eagle is the most dominant of all winged creatures. It soars higher than any bird on the planet. They are the rulers of the sky and convey power and messages of the spirit from the heavens.

Eagles symbolize strength, power, rebirth, renewal, courage and greatness! An ego is a person's sense of self-esteem or self-worth.

"Ladies, *stroke his eagle (ego) til the feathers fall off.*" – Clarissa

In life, you can hear all sorts of negative things about yourself whether they are true or not. But as humans, we can disregard what others think or say about us. Yet when it comes from a significant other, we are more than likely going to believe whatever it is that person says because we trust their judgement.

With that being said, wives, speak life into your husband! Husbands, speak life into your wives! Treat her like the Queen she is and nothing less. Talk to her with a kind, soft and sweet tone. Never belittle her. Never make her feel ugly or less than another woman! Marriage is all about building and growing together!

The master bedroom, or in the privacy of one another, is also the only acceptable place for quarrels. Never battle your spouse around other people or with other people in the mix. Never degrade one another during an argument. Never get physical with one another during an argument.

8) **Master bathroom**- The first object one observes upon entering a bathroom is the mirror. Most bathroom mirrors house a cabinet where medicine may be stored.

Illnesses in marriage are important to be mindful about. There are countless people, married and unmarried, living with natural born illnesses, physically disabling illnesses, invisible illnesses, etc.

Most wedding vows say, "Through sickness and in health". If your spouse has a sickness in his/her body, care for them as you'd desire them to care for you. Seek coping strategies geared towards that health issue.

When it comes to sickness of a child or a family member, it's safe to assume that one would want the spouse to be there in the physical with that family member. Well, hate to be the bearer of bad news, that is not always the case.

We've learned, through a close family member, that everyone copes differently with illness. Some truly can't stomach the agony it brings to watch a loved one suffer. This is where communication, sacrificing, compromising and balance comes into play.

Cleanliness is imperative in the master bathroom. The bathroom itself should be clean however, with women and their extra additional ventures on getting ready, that is not always the case.

Hair and make-up, for those that wear it, can be time consuming and not always quick to clean. Men, be patient with women like me!

Hygiene should always be a priority for both husband and wife. There are some cultures that have opposing views on what determines personal hygiene. To each its own!

Men, just a friendly reminder while we're in the bathroom, let's remember to put those toilet seats down! And a common courtesy for all, *"If you sprinkle when you twinkle, be a sweetie and wipe the seatie."* – Author Unknown

9) **Kids room**- The first thing that comes to mind when we step foot into kid's room is conception. For the couples trying to conceive that are having fertility dilemmas, we touch and agree right now that God sanctify your wound and give you the desires of your heart.

   Read the biblical story on Sarah and Abraham. May that be a reminder that God has the last say so on what can happen.

   The next thought of being in a kids room is pregnancy. Woman are beyond amazing for their ability to not only carry a child for nine months, but to actually give birth. It's a breathtaking site to see, literally!

   This is Rome talking to the husbands. When your wife carries your child, accept and embrace the physical changes in her body. As difficult as it can be, embrace her emotional state and her needy ways no matter how much she gets on your nerves.

   The hormonal changes may cause her to be emotional, angry, and joyful at the same time but continue to nurture her and support her the entire way through.

   Pass the pregnancy stage, parenting can be challenging in a marriage. Husbands and wives don't always see eye to eye for some odd reason when it comes to the kids.

   One important tip for married couples is not to correct one another in front of the kids. When you disagree with a parenting style, you wait until the kids aren't present. Doing so when they are present can discredit one's parenting ability.

   Impart positivity at all cost in your kid(s). Invest in

them mentally and financially by teaching family values, morals, ethics, financial stability and more. Don't wait until a situation occurs to teach them, utilize all moments with kids as a learning opportunity.

10) **Kitchen**- As a double standard, women are presumed to be the cooks of the house. But what if she marries a chef? Is he not supposed to utilize his expertise or passion for cooking to allow his wife to cook as her "duty"? Absolutely not!

This is yet another, "to each its own" and "whatever floats your boat" type of situation. Regardless of who does the cooking, healthiness and clean eating should be a regular practice and if it's not, it should be a goal to all couples.

When I met Rome, I was clueless to cooking! I had only prepared a few breakfast items and simple things like hamburger patties and French fries.

I had touched raw meat before, cooked anything in hot grease or even cook basic things like rice or potatoes. Rome, along with my sisters, mother and grandmothers, taught me just about everything I know.

Funny story. When we first got together, I was planning to make sloppy joes. As I begin to cook them, I realized that there was no ground beef in the can. When I expressed it to Rome, he took it as a joke, literally.

I didn't know that the canned Sloppy Joes is only a sauce! I assumed it was ready to good but apparently not. This is something that we've laughed about over the years.

Clean eating or the avoidance of processed food helps the immune system, reduce the risk of diabetes as well as cardiovascular disease, cancer, and ultimately can prolong life which gives you more time with your significant other on this side of heaven.

Making healthier choices is something we've incorporated in our lives for a small period of time. It started of with Rome and he's influenced me to eat healthier and avoid foods/beverages that aren't good to consume. So far, so good!

While we're in the kitchen, here's another friendly reminder about the garbage bag challenge unless it's never been an issue.

Home Setting

I'd be biased to say that it was the wife's duty to control the environment or atmosphere in the house. Something one may say or do sets the tone in a home.

Setting the tone creates the way activity thrive, especially the mood of the people whether it be spouse, kids, other live-in relatives or house guests.

For us as believers in Christ, we often pray for and seek out peace in our home. When you are at peace, positive energy naturally gravitates to you. You don't want the kids and or spouse to have to take a deep breath and "dive in" when entering the home.

No one should dread walking into their castle, entering upon their throne, or arriving at their headquarters. When entering our house, it's usually a warming, welcoming, tone. Set the tone for relaxation, tone for peace, tone for positive energy. "Positive vibes only" should be in lieu of a welcome mat upon entry of one's home.

We created ways to attract positive energy for those that may be conditioned to allowing the tone to be set based off one's mood or emotions. This should never be the case when it comes to home settings.

Ever notice how one thing goes wrong and it's a chain reaction, one thing after another? You wake on the wrong side of the bed, the kids bus doesn't come, you hit your toe, can't find your hair brush, car won't start, passwords won't work, bank account overdraft, menstrual start; it's emotionally draining and can ruin an entire day or week.

You look forward to and accept an array of bad things to happen. When I have these moments, I simply say "Not today devil!" For this very reason, we created our own ways to attract positive energy.

10 Ways to Attract Positive Energy

1) *Pray* - This concept is a personal favorite for us. Being believers in Christ and the Holy Bible, we stand firmly on faith that communicating with God brings forth a positive energy and peace that surpasses all! The bible tells us that the effectual fervent prayers of the righteous availeth much and in Matthew 7:7 *"Ask and it shall be given unto you, seek and you shall find, knock and the door will be opened to you."*...

2) *Meditate*- Meditation is a form or practice to create peace by achieving a mentally clear and emotionally calm state. It clears the mind, reduce stress and helps with relaxation. It's a worry-free time. There are various forms of meditation from religious and spiritual meditation to transcendental meditation.

3) *Workout/go for a walk* - Epinephrine known as adrenaline, is a hormone secreted by the adrenal glands which is released during moments of stress on the body both physically and emotionally.

An adrenaline rush triggers response throughout the body, including the release of neurotransmitters. Triggered by the rush, neurotransmitters called endorphins evoke an uplifting emotional response within the brain and help fight off the ill effects of stress. It's been known for doctors to prescribe exercise to help with depression and stress because of the emotional balance that adrenaline rushes provide.

4) *Listen to uplifting music*- Whether it be spiritual, contemporary, jazz, etc., indulge in your favorite tune. Try something with a positive message or soothing sounds. Music has always been known to be uplifting and to set a positive atmosphere.

5) *Focus*- It's awesome to have a peripheral vision type of focus in life. It helps you multi-task. There comes a time when you have to close in and focus on one task, idea, or event to avoid an overload. You don't always give your all when you have lots of other things that require your undivided attention.

6) *Omit Problems:* Although it is a healthy concept to admit problems in life, to attract positive energy and dwell in such a jaunty place, there are times where we have to overlook or omit our problems. We give too much thought in to issues and it can in turn, be depressing and put you in a negative filled place.

A prayer to help one omit their problems is the Serenity prayer. It reads, "*God, grant me the serenity to accept the things I cannot change, courage to change the things I can, and wisdom to know the difference.*"

There's a time and place, so to say, to address issues. When things are beyond your control, don't allow it to control you. There's a classic quote by Vivian Greene that says, "*Life isn't about waiting for the storm to pass, it's about learning to dance in the rain.*"

7) *Execute a hobby*- Doing something that you show interest in or partake in a hobby can give off an ecstatic feeling.

Whether its reading, writing, painting, pottery, dancing, couponing, playing musical instruments, knitting- the list of hobbies can go on and on. When you demonstrate these things that you typically excel at, it puts forth a positive energy of self-satisfaction for accomplishing something.

8) *Reflect*- Reflection journals are a writer's best friend! Many writers use a reflective journal to keep track of progress or occurrences during a particular timeframe or experience. These personal records may be used as a precedent for similar encounters in the future. One may also mentally or verbally reflect to attract positive energy. Via testimonies of overcoming situations brings gratitude for the present. Gratitude conveys into that positive energy.

9) *Laugh a little*- Tell a joke, watch a comedy, etc... Simple, laughter is good for the soul!

10) *Speak positivity*- Literally, speak positivity in the atmosphere. The bible says in Proverbs 18:21 *"Death and life are in the power of the tongue: and they that every day and even throughout the day, speak positivity in your life."*

Work, home, school, with your kids, friends, family members, and in your relationship and marriage. Read motivational quotes. Create mantras. Explore various proverbs. Reframe your mindset by using mantras on a regular.

Marriage mantras are simple words or phrases that have the authority to interrupt all negative forces in your marriage. Memorize them, meditate on them, but most of all, believe them!

Sit with your spouse and discuss mantras relating to your marriage in particular. By nature, the positive mantras will manifest. You may even be one to explore chanting mantras which falls under Hindu and Buddhist mantras. Pinterst.com also has a variety of ideas on how to create and utilize mantras.

Here are some of our marriage mantras…
* *Hard times*: We were built for this!
* *Growth*: Skies the limit!
* *Love*: Like there's no tomorrow.
* *Vow*: Until death do us part.
* *Communication*: Listen twice as much as you speak.
* *Peace*: Be still!
* *Struggle*: Keep pressing!

If you're like us and work at a desk, frame some of these positive quotes, scriptures or mantras to attract positive energy at work. An all-time favorite is…

"Attitudes are contagious. Make yours worth catching."
–Clarissa Green

SOCIAL MEDIA

Over the past two decades, social media has evolved into an incredible, premier source of communication globally. It's a part of many people's, including ours, daily life. From chatting, sharing information, entertainment, and virtual reality of just about anything one can think of; It has become the modern day television, news center and telephone all in one.

One may portray themselves as something or someone they're not solely for popularity, 'likes', shares and even to cause an uproar to go viral on social media.

Social media connects the world from high end corporate and politicians, to every day nine to five workers and the homeless with users of all ages across the globe.

Studies shows that social media has damaging effects for many reasons. It highly influences ones' truth, reality and depicts what is natural and what is artificial. In a relationship or marriage, social media can have an impact on one's life and how we perceive things.

Contrary to popular belief, common sense is not that common! There are countless topics via social media pertaining to marriages and relationships in which there is either no common denominator or some just find it necessary to disagree.

Below are some common martial questions that emerged from social media followed by our response. These questions have been "*BANNED*" from certain social media groups related to marriage due to their irrelevance, irrational responses, and the fact that there is no 'one size fits all' in answering.

1. *Who eats first? Husband or kids?*
   *Answer: **NOT APPLICABLE!** The kid's plates are typically made first, so they may cool down a bit. Rome likes his plate nice and hot straight from the stove! Most of the time, we all sit together in the living room and eat. By God's grace, no one has had to go hungry in our household, God provides more than enough for us *all* to eat.

2. *If there was an argument and your husband tell you to go to the car and dad says, 'sit down', who do you listen to?*
   *Answer: **HUSBAND**. This is a scenario that I'd never expect to happen. My dad knows the significance of marriage and I can't imagine him ever intervening and making me choose who to "obey". He instills in us to submit to our husbands. If it ever happened, I'd politely kiss daddy on the cheek, say "I love you" and stroll my pigeon-toed tail to the car!

3. *If your husband's baby mother was on bus stop with their child while it was snowing, what do you do?*
   *Answer: Offer **THEM** a ride. First of all, it's neglect if you keep it moving. It's childish and petty if you attempt to get the child and leave the mother. This is one of those situations where you must be cordial.

4. *Is it appropriate for a woman to propose to a man?*
   *Answer: **NO!** A proposal is asking someone to take your hand in marriage. The bible says, "HE who finds a WIFE finds a good thing" not the other way around.

5. *Is it okay for a step parent to physically punish a step child?*
   *Answer: **DEPENDS**. I'd probably say yes to a live in, parent-figure step parent. No to the every now and again, every other weekend type of step parent.

6. *Should a husband defend his wife from insults from his family?*
   *Answer: **YES**! Even though "blood is thicker than water", a spouse is one with you, it's your other half. A husband should never allow anyone (**no exclusions**) to insult or talk bad about his wife without defending her.

7. *Is it okay to go through your spouse phone?*
   *Answer: **YES**! Privacy is not who you call and text. Privacy is letting you watch the football game or soap operas with no interruptions! Know the difference.

8. *Who comes first in a man's life? Wife, mother, baby mama, or daughter?*
   *Answer: **DEPENDS**. Well, let's start by saying a baby mama is, without a doubt, not in the category of importance with mom, wife and daughter. A wife is one with the husband, a daughter belongs to the both and a mil or mother in law is both of their mothers. We all only get one mother, so a wife just may have to compromise, to a certain degree, and allow a husband's mother to go ahead of her.

9. *Is it okay to serve a husband his dinner on a plastic or paper plate?*
   *Answer: **YES**! If he has some type of bitterness towards paper/plastic plate, then sure, feed him from a glass plate. But plastic or paper doesn't diminish the taste or value of the meal.

10. *Would you deactivate your social media page(s) to save your marriage?*
    *Answer: **ABSOLUTELY**! Social media serves as a moderate intensity of importance outside of pleasure. It serves as networking and business as well. If it causes chaos in a marriage, yes it can be sacrificed.

11. *Would you say yes if your husband proposes with a small or "cheap" looking wedding ring?*
    *Answer: **YES**! As stated at the beginning of this book, a ring is symbolic, the commitment is what's relevant. However, if it's purchased when funds are not an issue then we may have a problem!

12. *Is it okay for a wife to have a "work husband" and/or a husband to have a "work wife"?*
    *Answer: Absolutely **NOT**! We're stuck trying to figure out why this is even a thing! Co-workers are co-workers! Co-workers may buy each other lunch, coffee, help each other with work but it's not appropriate to consider a co-worker a "work spouse."

13. *Ladies, your man invites you to his grandma's house for Thanksgiving and she also invites his ex. His ex-girlfriend fixes him a plate, what do you do?*
    *Answer: **EAT** from our plate! When we said our vows, we became one. She made OUR plate, not just his plate! I'd politely say thanks and get first dibs as I always do with his meals.

14. *Should you and your spouse share Facebook/social media pages?*
    *Answer: **Does not matter.** We have our own social media pages. We wouldn't care if we did share. Having different type of audiences will be agitating.

And the fact that we'd have to add our personal name behind a comment would be annoying!

15. The **ULTIMATE** social media ban is from all the wives in the world.
    Answer: "Hell no, my husband is not allowed to wear sweats!" This is a universal ban in which husbands have absolutely no say so! Sweats or jogging pants have been known to attract eyes near the crotch area. A man's, or at the least my husband's, privacy imprint is in no way, shape, form or fashion acceptable for the public's view.

As fun as it was answering those questions, they were still answered truthfully. You may agree with some, you may agree with all, but I can guarantee you, you will agree with most!

Set standards and boundaries on social media together. Never directly or indirectly bash your spouse or marriage. One must realize, once it's on the internet, it can't be deleted. You're also setting the social atmosphere of how others should see or address you and your marriage.

Hashtags, formerly known as the number or pound sign, are taking the world by storm! For those that didn't know, you can type in # in a search engine on social media or the internet followed by a word, topic or group of words and get a list of posts relating to that hashtag.

One of my all-time favorites is #MarriageGoals. All married couples should have or create goals together. It's not only fun, but it's exciting to achieve them together. Need a jump? Utilize some of the ones listed below.

1) Read "*The Ring* by Mr. & Mrs. Green" together, as a unit.
2) Create vision boards.
3) Grow. Mature. Inspire.

4) Set career goals. Whether it's work related or one furthering their education.
5) Build an empire. Launch a business, build/buy a house, etc.
6) Start a family. Have a kid or two, adopt a child, or get a pet.
7) Financial freedom- Aim to be debt free. Build your credit. Pour into savings: 401k, CD's, stocks and bonds, etc.
8) Reach for longevity. Grow old and gray together.
9) Attend church together.
10) Uplift one another regularly. Compliment daily. Speak life into one another. Encourage each other
11) Establish routines.
12) Always show love and affection. Never let it fade.
13) Cherish every moment, create memories.
14) Travel. Explore. Be adventurous
15) Get fit. Be healthy.

"The goal in a marriage is not to think alike, but to think together." - Robert C. Dodds

"I DO!" OR… "DO I?"

The basic, non-denominational, traditional marriage vows are the "Question of Intention" and the "Standard Civil Ceremony". The "Question of Intention", adapted from the traditional Medieval Christian ceremony, commences with the officiant performing the ceremony asking the couple to join hands before asking each, groom first, the following:

"[Name], do you take [Name] to be your wedded [husband/wife] to live together in marriage? Do you promise to love, comfort, honor and keep [him/her]? For better or worse, for richer or poorer, in sickness and in health? And forsaking all others, be faithful only to [him/her] so long as you both shall live?"

Which is answered by "*I do.*" The official then asks the other spouse the same thing and they too reply, "*I do.*" Then they are pronounced husband and wife by the power vested in him or her (the officiant).

This chapter will be based on traditional wedding vows, not by other denominations or vows written specifically for a husband and wife.

In a marriage, I'm almost positive that at some point or another, the '*I Do!*' exclamatory oath can resort to the uncertainty turning it into the question '*Do I?*'.

The uncertainty of if being married to someone was the right thing to do usually arise during a situation or from multiple occurrences building up. When a commitment, loyalty, trust or vows are broken, how do you still preserve an "*I do!*" mindset?

Think back to that initial wedding vow. At what point did it say that there wouldn't be stumbling blocks, bad days, disagreements? I'm sure you'll never locate it.

Wherever there is a "good thing", the devil will always be on the prowl seeking after someone to devour! If your marriage is ordained by God, you are a target on satan's hit-list!

Marriage is and has always been under attack by the world. It takes two to endure the hardships that may come in a marriage. As stated in the Foreword, marriage is continuous work. It's bound to be tried by the fire, but the beautifully scoped diamonds can glisten and supersede all hindrances.

Someone on social media said, "*Marriage is cheap… Divorce is expensive… Freedom is priceless.*"

Then someone's perfect response was, "*Marriage is not cheap. It's a high price to pay if done correctly and divorce is not even an option so it's expense is not even considered. But the only way this is possible is by both parties being joined to Christ Jesus who is the head of their union.*" I couldn't agree more with this response!

We speak prosperity over all the marriages that encounter this book. We pray that whatever obstacles you all are facing, that complete healing takes place! Our hopes are that something, if not all, in this book encourage, uplift, motivate, cultivate and strengthen your union.

May all your questionable "*Do I?*" defer to the exclamatory phase of "*I DO!*"

WEDDING VOWS

Just wanted to share some fun facts regarding other cultures may relay their wedding vow.

Source: https://www.theknot.com/content/traditional-wedding-vows-from-various-religions
By: From Rev. Edward Searl, Unitarian Church of Hinsdale, IL

Protestant Wedding Vows
There are many different types of Protestant churches, all with their own slightly different traditions and beliefs. Below are typical vows from various denominations, but you'll find many of them differ only slightly from one another.

Basic Protestant Vows
"I, ___, take thee, ___, to be my wedded husband/wife, to have and to hold, from this day forward, for better, for worse, for richer, for poorer, in sickness and in health, to love and to cherish, till death do us part, according to God's holy ordinance; and thereto I pledge thee my faith [or] pledge myself to you."

Episcopal
"____, wilt thou have this woman/man to be thy wedded wife/husband to live together after God's ordinance in the Holy Estate of matrimony? Wilt thou love her/him? Comfort her/him, honor and keep her/him, in sickness and in health, and forsaking all others keep thee only unto her/him as long as you both shall live?"

"In the name of God, I, _____, take you, _____, to be my wife/husband, to have and to hold from this day forward, for better, for worse, for richer, for poorer, in sickness and health, to love and to cherish, until we are parted by death. This is my solemn vow."

Methodist

"Will you have this woman/man to be your wife/husband, to live together in holy marriage? Will you love her/him, comfort her/him, honor, and keep her/him in sickness and in health, and forsaking all others, be faithful to her/him as long as you both shall live?"

"In the name of God, I, _____, take you, _____, to be my wife/husband, to have and to hold from this day forward, for better, for worse, for richer, for poorer, in sickness and in health, to love and to cherish, until we are parted by death. This is my solemn vow."

Presbyterian

"_____, wilt thou have this woman/man to be thy wife/husband, and wilt thou pledge thy faith to him/her, in all love and honor, in all duty and service, in all faith and tenderness, to live with her/him, and cherish her/him, according to the ordinance of God, in the holy bond of marriage?"

"I, _____, take you, _____, to be my wedded wife/husband, and I do promise and covenant, before God and these witnesses, to be your loving and faithful husband/wife, in plenty and want, in joy and in sorrow, in sickness and in health, as long as we both shall live."

Lutheran

"I take you, _____, to be my wife/husband from this day forward, to join with you and share all that is to come, and I promise to be faithful to you until death parts us."

"I, _____, take you, _____, to be my wife/husband, and these things I promise you: I will be faithful to you and honest with you; I will respect, trust, help, and care for you; I will share my life with you; I will forgive you as we have been forgiven; and I will try with you better to understand ourselves, the world and God; through the best and worst of what is to come, and as long as we live."

Catholic Wedding Vows
"I, ___, take you, ___, for my lawful wife/husband, to have and to hold from this day forward, for better, for worse, for richer, for poorer, in sickness and health, until death do us part."

"I, ___, take you, ___, to be my husband/wife. I promise to be true to you in good times and in bad, in sickness and in health. I will love and honor you all the days of my life."

Hindu Wedding Vows
Traditional Hindu wedding ceremonies have many elements and rituals. Technically there are no "vows" in the Western sense, but the Seven Steps, or Saptha Padhi, around a flame (honoring the fire god, Agni) spell out the promises the couple makes to each other:

"Let us take the first step to provide for our household a nourishing and pure diet, avoiding those foods injurious to healthy living.

"Let us take the second step to develop physical, mental and spiritual powers.

"Let us take the third step to increase our wealth by righteous means and proper use.

"Let us take the fourth step to acquire knowledge, happiness and harmony by mutual love and trust.

"Let us take the fifth step so that we are blessed with strong, virtuous and heroic children.

"Let us take the sixth step for self-restraint and longevity.

"Finally, let us take the seventh step and be true companions and remain lifelong partners by this wedlock."

Jewish Wedding Vows

In a traditional Jewish ceremony, there is no actual exchange of vows; the covenant is said to be implicit in the ritual. The Jewish wedding ceremony structure varies within Orthodox, Conservative, Reform and Reconstructionist synagogues, and also among individual rabbis. The marriage vow is customarily sealed when the groom places a ring on the bride's finger and says (in English transliteration), "Haray at mekudeshet lee beh-taba'at zo keh-dat Moshe veh-Yisrael," which translates to, "Behold, you are consecrated to me with this ring according to the laws of Moses and Israel."

Many Jewish couples today do want to exchange spoken vows; they are now included in many Reform and Conservative ceremonies.

Example of Reform Vows
"Do you,___, take____ to be your wife/husband, promising to cherish and protect her/him, whether in good fortune or in adversity, and to seek together with her/him a life hallowed by the faith of Israel?"

Example of Conservative Vows
"Do you, ___, take ____ to be your lawfully wedded wife/husband, to love, to honor and to cherish?"

Another version of nontraditional vows is a phrase from the Song of Songs: "Ani leh-dodee veh-dodee lee," which means, "I am my beloved's, and my beloved is mine."

Muslim Wedding Vows
Most Muslim couples do not recite vows, but rather heed the words of the imam (cleric), who speaks about the meaning of marriage and the couple's responsibilities to each other and to Allah during the nikah, or marriage contract. At the end of this ritual, the couple consents to become husband and wife, and they are blessed by the congregation. However, some Muslim brides and grooms do recite vows -- here is a common

recitation:

Bride: "I, __, offer you myself in marriage in accordance with the instructions of the Holy Quran and the Holy Prophet, peace and blessing be upon him. I pledge, in honesty and with sincerity, to be for you an obedient and faithful wife." Groom: "I pledge, in honesty and sincerity, to be for you a faithful and helpful husband."

Eastern Orthodox Wedding Vows
Ceremony- an introspective prayer in which the couple promises to be loyal and loving to each other. In the Russian tradition, however, vows are spoken out loud:

"I, __, take you, __, as my wedded wife/husband and I promise you love, honor and respect; to be faithful to you, and not to forsake you until death do us part. So, help me God, one in the Holy Trinity and all the Saints."

Nondenominational Wedding Vows
"I, ____, take you, ____, to be no other than yourself. Loving what I know of you, trusting what I do not yet know, I will respect your integrity and have faith in your abiding love for me, through all our years, and in all that life may bring us."

"____, I take you as my wife/husband, with your faults and your strengths, as I offer myself to you with my faults and my strengths. I will help you when you need help and turn to you when I need help. I choose you as the person with whom I will spend my life."

Quaker
"In the presence of God and these our friends I take thee, ____, to be my husband/wife, promising with Divine assistance to be unto thee a loving and faithful husband/wife so long as we both shall live."

NCADV: Facts about Domestic Violence and Physical Abuse

https://www.speakcdn.com/assets/2497/domestic_violence_and_physical_abuse_ncadv.pdf

WHAT IS INTIMATE PARTNER PHYSICAL ABUSE?
Physical abuse includes the physical assault, battery, and sexual assault used as part of a systematic pattern of power and control perpetrated by one intimate partner against another. Physical abuse can cause severe injury and even death. It often co-occurs with other forms of abuse, including psychological abuse, economic abuse, and stalking.

INTIMATE PARTNER PHYSICAL ABUSE:
- More than 10 million Americans are victims of physical violence annually.
- 20 people are victims of physical violence every minute in the United States.
- 1 in 3 women and 1 in 4 men is a victim of some form of physical violence by an intimate partner during their lifetimes.
- 76% of intimate partner physical violence victims are female; 24% are male.
- 1 in 7 women and 1 in 18 men are severely injured by intimate partners in their lifetimes.
- Domestic violence accounts for 15% of all violent crime in the United States.
- Domestic violence is most common among women aged 18-24 and 25-34.
- A majority of physical abuse is committed by dating partners rather than spouses.
- More than 75% of women aged 18-49 who are abused were previously abused by the same perpetrator.
- Intimate partner physical abuse has declined 67% since the passage of the Violence Against Women Act in 1994.

- Slightly more than half of intimate partner physical violence is reported to law enforcement.

INTIMATE PARTNER HOMICIDE:
- In 2007, 1,640 women were murdered by intimate partners; in 2012, 924 women were killed by intimate partners.
- 40% of female murder victims are killed by intimate partners.
- Almost half of intimate partner homicides are committed by dating partners.
- 76% of women who are killed by intimate partners and 85% of women who survive homicide attempts are stalked prior to the murder or attempted murder.

WHY DOES IT MATTER?
Intimate partner physical abuse is not bound by age, socioeconomic status, race, ethnicity, sex, sexual orientation, gender identity, religion or nationality; it exists in all communities. Contrary to popular belief, physical abuse is not simply a maladjusted person's occasional expression of frustration or anger, nor is it typically an isolated incident. Physical abuse is a tool of control and oppression and is a choice made by one person in a relationship to control another.

OTHER FORMS OF ABUSE
SEXUAL ASSAULT:
- 1 in 5 women and 1 in 59 men in the United States is raped during his/her lifetime.
- 9.4% of women in the United States have been raped by an intimate partner.

STALKING:
- 19.3 million women and 5.1 million men in the United States have been stalked.
- 66.2% of female stalking victims reported stalking by a current or former intimate partner.

HOMICIDE:
- 1 in 3 female murder victims and 1 in 20 male murder victims are killed by intimate partners.
- A study of intimate partner homicides found 20% of victims were family members or friends of the abused partner, neighbors, persons who intervened, law enforcement responders, or bystanders.
- 72% of all murder-suicides are perpetrated by intimate partners.
- 94% of murder-suicide victims are female.
- 19.3 million women and 5.1 million men in the United States have been stalked.
- 66.2% of female stalking victims reported stalking by a current or former intimate partner.

HOMICIDE:
- 1 in 3 female murder victims and 1 in 20 male murder victims are killed by intimate partners.
- A study of intimate partner homicides found 20% of victims were family members or friends of the abused partner, neighbors, persons who intervened, law enforcement responders, or bystanders.
- 72% of all murder-suicides are perpetrated by intimate partners.
- 94% of murder-suicide victims are female.

If you need help: Call The National Domestic Violence Hotline   1-800-799-SAFE (7233) Or, online go to DomesticShelters.org

Mr. & Mrs. Green

ABOUT THE AUTHORS

Romaro Green
Inspired by God and influenced by his wife, Romaro was compelled to use his God given gift to make room for him. For the past few years, he's conducted ministry beyond the pulpit including the harsh streets of Milwaukee, WI, hospitals rooms, weddings, funerals and social media. He's allowed the social media platform to expand his reach on the lives he touches through encouraging words, uplifting advice and by answering a magnitude of prayer request.

Clarissa Green
As the owner and operated of Unbreakable Publishing Company, Clarissa's focus with ministry has been to help others break barriers and overcome obstacles. Coming from a "broken home" with little to no stability and guidance, she's set out to aid others in similar situations by focusing on growth and development, empowerment while striving for excellence and beating the odds.

This book is available for purchase at the following:

Available at www.createspace.com/8024677
Available on Amazon.com
Available on Amazon Europe
Or Contact the publisher at Unbreakablepub@yahoo.com

For booking information or exclusive interviews,
please contact the publisher/author at:
Unbreakablepub@yahoo.com

www.ingramcontent.com/pod-product-compliance
Lightning Source LLC
Chambersburg PA
CBHW050652160426
43194CB00010B/1912